Saffell Charles C.

The Citizen Soldiers at North Point and Port McHenry, September 12 and 13, 1814.

Resolves of the citizens in town meeting, particulars relating to the battle, official correspondence and honorable discharge of the troops.

Saffell Charles C.

The Citizen Soldiers at North Point and Port McHenry, September 12 and 13, 1814.
Resolves of the citizens in town meeting, particulars relating to the battle, official correspondence and honorable discharge of the troops.

ISBN/EAN: 9783337308216

Printed in Europe, USA, Canada, Australia, Japan

Cover: Foto ©ninafisch / pixelio.de

More available books at **www.hansebooks.com**

THE

CITIZEN SOLDIERS

AT

NORTH POINT AND FORT McHENRY,

SEPTEMBER 12 & 13,

1814.

RESOLVES OF THE CITIZENS IN TOWN MEETING, PARTICULARS
RELATING TO THE BATTLE, OFFICIAL CORRESPONDENCE
AND HONORABLE DISCHARGE OF THE TROOPS.

ALSO,
CELEBRATION OF THE SEVENTY-FIFTH ANNIVERSARY, 1889.
REPRINT.

CHARLES C. SAFFELL,
BALTIMORE, MD.

TO THE MEMORY

OF THE

GALLANT AND LAMENTED

MAJ. GEN. SAMUEL SMITH,

THE HERO OF TWO WARS,

AN ENLIGHTENED STATESMAN AND AN HONEST AGENT, WHOSE DAYS FROM THE EARLIEST PERIOD OF MANHOOD TO UPWARDS OF FOURSCORE YEARS, WAS DEVOTED TO HIS COUNTRY AND HIS COUNTRY'S GOOD: TO HIM, AND TO THE CITIZEN SOLDIERY WHO SERVED WITH HIM AT THE PERIOD HEREIN REFERRED TO, THIS WORK IS RESPECTFULLY INSCRIBED BY

THE PUBLISHER.

ADVERTISEMENT.

In the compilation of this volume, the publisher has been guided by no other wish than to present a correct and impartial statement of the various Divisions, Brigades, Regiments and Companies, with the rank of every citizen who had the honor of serving his country on the twelfth and thirteenth of September, 1814, at North Point and Fort McHenry.

The extracts are copied from the original rolls on file in the 3d auditor's office of the War Department, and should errors occur in any of the companies, by the insertion of the names of individuals who were not present at the battle, or by the non-appearance of others, and by the varied rank of any of the officers, the error must be attributed to their own accounting officer, and be satisfied that it was the wish of no one to hold back the services of any, or to add any renown where it did not justly belong.

The publisher also regrets his inability to obtain anything like correct information respecting the Virginia and Baltimore County troops—as soon as received, it will be printed.

MUSTER ROLL.

Names of the General and Staff Officers of the third Division of Maryland Militia in the service of the United States on the 12th day of September, 1814:

SAMUEL SMITH, *Major General.*
ISAAC MCKIM, *Aid-de-Camp.*
EDWARD PATTERSON, *Aid-de-Camp.*
JOHN SPEAR SMITH, *Volunteer Aid.*
JONATHAN MEREDITH, *Division Inspector.*
WILLIAM BATES, *Ass't Adjutant General.*
ROBERT PATTERSON, *Ass't Division Inspector.*
JEREMIAH SULLIVAN, *Division Quarter Master.*
NICHOLAS PRICE, *Special Judge Advocate.*
ROBERT S. HOLLIS, *Secretary to the General.*

Names of the General and Staff Officers of the 11th Brigade third Division of Maryland Militia in the service of the United States on the 12th September, 1814:

TOBIAS E. STANSBURY, *Brigadier General.*
JAMES HASLETT, *Brigade Major.*
EDWARD G. WOODYEAR, *Aid-de-Camp.*
JOHN NELSON, *1st Lieut. and Ass't Aid-de-Camp.*
GEORGE HARRYMAN, *Brigade Quarter Master.*
GEORGE FISHER, *Wagon Master.*
WESLEY WALKER, *Forage Master.*

Names of the General and Staff Officers of the first Brigade of Maryland Militia in the service of the United States on the 12th day of September, 1814:

THOMAS FORMAN, *Brigadier General.*
PHILIP THOMAS, *Aid-de-Camp.*
R. W. ARMSTRONG, *Brigade Major.*
SAMUEL BRADFORD, *Brigade Quarter Master.*
THOMAS BROWN, *Brigade Wagon Master.*

Names of the General and Staff Officers of the third Brigade of Maryland Militia in the service of the United States on the 12th of September, 1814:

JOHN STRICKER, *Brigadier General.*
JAMES CALHOUN, JR., *Brigade Major.*
GEORGE P. STEVENSON, *Aid-de-Camp.*
JACOB SMALL, *Brigade Quarter Master.*

Names of the Field and Staff and Company Officers, Non-Commissioned Officers, and Privates of the fifth Regiment of Maryland Cavalry Militia, who served at North Point and Fort McHenry, 12th September, 1814, taken from the Muster Rolls on file in the office of the Third Auditor of the Treasury of the United States:

JAMES BIAYS, *Lieutenant Colonel.*
WILLIAM JACKSON, *1st Major.*
WILLIAM B. BARNEY, *2d Major.*
LEMUEL TAYLOR, *Adjutant.*
F. C. TOELLE, *Surgeon.*
CAMPBELL P. WHITE, *Quarter Master.*
JOHN HASLAM, *Veterinary Surgeon.*
JAMES BLAIR, *Sergeant Major.*

INDEPENDENT LIGHT DRAGOONS.

Jehu Bouldin, Captain.
Thomas Kell, 1st Lieut.
Joseph R. Foard, 2d Lieut.
Nath'l Hitchcock, Cornet.
Samuel Alberger, 1st Sergt.
John Carnoles, 2d do.

Eli Green,	3d Ser'gt.	Gambril, John	Private.
Fer'd. Brushweller,	4th do.	Gill, Bennet C.	"
Nathaniel Smith,	1st Corp'l.	Green, Abed	"
William Thomas,	2d do.	Henwood, Joshua	"
William Mumma,	3d do.	Hall, Caleb	"
James C. Dew,	4th do.	Mumma, John	"
John Buck, Trumpeter.		Mumma, Henry	"
Cross William S.	Private.	Maxfield, John	"
Coats, Frederick	"	McGlennan, James	"
Cristmond, Thomas	"	McLaughlin, Daniel	"
Davis, Amos	"	Newton, Anthony	"
Denny, David G.	"	O'Riety, Joseph C.	"
Everet, Thomas	"	Reese, Henry	"
Gill, Nicholas C.	"		

FIRST BALTIMORE HUSSARS.

James Sterett, Captain.		Griffith, Samuel G.	Private.
John Smith Hollins, 1st Lieut.		Hurxthall, Ferdinand	"
John W. Stump,	2d do.	Herring, Henry	"
James Barroll, Cornet.		Hollingsworth, Sam'l, jr.	"
Wesley Woods, Q. M. S.		Hollins, William	"
Peter Delvachio,	1st Ser'gt.	Levering, Francis	"
John Sterling,	2d do.	Ludden, Lemuel, jr.	"
Wm. B. Buchanan,	3d do.	Lorman, Alexander	"
Sam'l McClellan,	4th do.	Mulliken, Richard D.	"
Nath'l Saltenstal,	1st Corp'l.	Marean, Thomas	"
Francis Cooke,	2d do.	McNully, John	"
Eli Simpkins,	3d do.	Mahr Martin F,	"
Samuel Scott,	4th do.	Mulliken, Basil D.	"
Ailken Robert,	Private.	Marsh Stephen	"
Bowley, Samuel	"	Moshur, James, jr.	"
Belt, Thomas H.	"	McLannahan, J. J.	"
Binys, Philip	"	O'Donnell, Columbus	"
Boggs, Alexander L.	"	Owings, Beal	"
Benson, Robert	"	Partridge, James	"
Boehme, Charles L.	"	Palmer, Edward	"
Boyle, Hugh	"	Price, Walter	"
Cox, James jr.	"	Prince, Caspar	"
Carroll, H. D. G.	"	Rogers, Henry W.	"
Coulson, George	"	Raborg, Samuel	"
Carr, Thomas	"	Ricaud, Benjamin	"
Dorsey, Edward H.	"	Ridgate, Benjamin C.	"
Dorsey, Richard B.	"	Scott, Henry D.	"
Dorsey, Samuel	"	Sleeper, Jonathan	"
Evans, Hugh W.	"	Swann, John	"
Frisby, Richard	"	Stewart, Alexander	"
Gibson, John	"	Spillman, James	"
Gorsuch, Robert	"	Sterett, William	"
Gittings, James C.	"	Tschudy, Samuel	"
Gittings, James, jr.	"	Taylor, Lemuel G.	"

Van Wyck, John C.	Private.	Wallis, John, jr.	Private.
White, Joseph	"	Ward, Solomon	"
Wheeler, James B.	"	Wilkins, John	"
Williams, Henry L.	"	Wilkins, Joseph	"
Wilmer, John W.	"	Wireman, William	"
Waring, George W.	"	Yellott, George	"
Waters, Richard	"		

MARYLAND CHASSEURS.

James Horton, Captain.	Kirk, Thomas	Private.
Jacob Myers, Lieutenant.	Kohlstadt, Benjamin	"
Elijah Beam, do.	Lauduslager, Jacob	"
John Stierly, Cornet.	Levy, Andrew	"
Jacob Hanny, Sergeant.	Maidwell, John	"
Thomas Welsh, do.	Miller, Christopher	"
Wm. Stansbury, do.	Myers, Henry	"
Andrew Rohr, do.	Myers, William	"
Richard Grimes, do.	Marche, Perry	"
Caleb Turner, Corporal.	Mercer, James	"
John Craggs, do.	Ross, Thomas	"
Joseph Everson, do.	Storey, Robert	"
John Durham, do.	Seltzer, Jacob	"
Beam, William Private.	Seltzer, Lewis	"
Butler, James "	Sheffer, Jesse	"
Bankard, Jacob "	Simpson, John	"
Bower, Jacob "	Winnigden, Lewis	"
Foreman, Elijah "	Winkler, John	"
Fansbrimer, Daniel "	Wood, Henry H.	"
Fuller, Nicholas "	Walker, Sater T.	"
Gowan, John "	Willson, Greenbury	"
Hammer, George "	Zigler, John L.	"
Jackson, William "	Zigler, John W.	"
Krail, John G. "		

FELL'S POINT LIGHT DRAGOONS.

John Hanna, Captain.	Andrew Dalck, 1st Corp'l.	
John Rusk, 1st Lieut.	John Craig, 2d do.	
Peter Peduse, 2d do.	John Weedham, 3d do.	
Thomas Raven, Cornet.	Thomas Sprigg, 4th do.	
J. Shinnick, Co. Qr. Mr. Sgt.	Bryan, Charles	Private.
Henry Dorry, 1st Serg't.	Cole, Nathaniel	"
Calvin Cooper, 2d do.	Cassidy, Patrick	"
E. Galloway, 3d do.	Carroll, Patrick	"
Peter Cavana, 4th do.	Deal, George	"

Delcher, John	Private.	Pilch, James	Private.
Haeffer, Joel	"	Rush, George	"
Huster, Gotleib	"	Stansbury, Josias	"
Harryman Stephen	"	Stevenson, Joshua	"
McGinnis, John	"	Senton, Robert	"
McDonald, Hugh	"	Steine, George	"
Malloy, Patrick	"	Turner, Thomas	"
Patridge, Daubner B.	"		

Names of the Field and Staff and Company Officers, Non-Commissioned Officers and Privates of the First Regiment of Artillery of the Maryland Militia, who served at North Point and Fort McHenry on the 12th day of September, 1814, taken from the Muster Rolls on file in the office of the 3d Auditor of the Treasury of the United States.

DAVID HARRIS, *Lieutenant Colonel.*
SOLOMON G. ALBERS, 1st *Major.*
MATTHEW MCLAUGHLIN, 2d *do.*
UPTON S. HEATH, 1st *Lieutenant and Adjutant.*
BENJAMIN HODGES, 1st *Lieutenant and Pay Master.*
JOHN G. JOHNSTON, *Quarter Master.*
MARTIN FURWICK, *Surgeon.*
MICHAEL DIFFENDERFFER, *Surgeon's Mate.*
NATHANIEL PEARCE, *Sergeant Major.*
AUGUSTUS BAUGHAN, *Sergeant Major.*
JOHN THOMAS, *Quarter Master.*

FRANKLIN ARTILLERY.

Joseph Myers, Captain.	Bush, John F.	Private.
Lyman Adams, 1st Lieut.	Clifford, Sylvester	"
Julius Willard, 2d do.	Clark, William	"
William Miller, 3d do.	Cocur, John	"
And. McClellen, 1st Ser'gt.	Cochran, William A.	"
Thomas Stow, 2d do.	Fontz, Henry	"
Jno. H. Newman, 3d do.	Freeman, Charles	"
Ph. Buckingham, 4th do.	Forrester, Lenard	"
John Rogers, 1st Corp'l.	Gowen, George	"
John Wright, 2d do.	Haddaway, William	"
William Web, 3d do.	Hay, George	"
Isaac Baker, 4th do.	Hall, Eliga	"
John Simpson, Musician.	Hennaman, Isaac	"
Edward Thompson, do.	Henneman, Jacob	"
Boyd, Joseph Private.	Herbert, Charles	"
Berry, Thomas D. "	Howel, Abraham	"
Bangs, John "	Jordan, Henry	"
Basdey, James "	King, John	"

Kreigh, Frederick	Private.	Sunenshine, Michael	Private.
Kemp, William	"	Shumack, Stephen	"
Kennedy, Richard	"	Suter, Jacob	"
Lloyd, William	"	Stoudt, George	"
Matthews, Thomas L.	"	Slayton, David	"
Metzguer, William	"	Thompson, William	"
Moody, Isaac	"	Turner, Joseph	"
Martin, John	"	Worthan, Damon	"
McKim, Daniel	"	Walker, William	"
Mortimer, John	"	Wood, John G.	"
McGill, Arthur	"	Williams, Horatio	"
Notherman, George	"	Willis, Justan	"
Neal, Richard	"	White Henry,	"
Nicholson, William	"	Waters, Stephen	"
Oler, George	"	Waters, Joseph	"
Patterson, William	"	Weaver, Daniel	"
Price, Nehemiah	"	Whatkins, Gassway	"
Retew, William	"	Wiley, Robert	"
Stevenson, Isaiah		Zimmerman, John	"
Summerwell, Richard			

COLUMBIAN ARTILLERY.

Samuel Moale, Captain.	Deal, Jacob	Private
Barrack Williams, 1st Lieut.	Dunkel, E. A.	"
William Frick, 2d do.	Ducatel, J. F.	"
William Shroeder, 3d do.	Dalrymple, William P.	"
R. W. Latimer, 1st Ser'gt.	Dorsey, Hammond	"
James Sykes, 2d do.	Darvis, Edward	"
Wm. P. Lemmon, 3d do.	Finley, Ebenezer L.	"
Isaac C. Lea, 4th do.	Finlay, Hugh	"
Ebenezer Perkins, 1st Corp'l.	Golder, Archibald	"
Wm. Renshaw, 2d do.	Green, Thomas B.	"
John G. Comegys, 3d do.	Grafton, Nathan	"
Mathias Rich, 4th do.	Grafton, Mark	"
Thomas Whitlow, Drummer.	Gill, John B.	"
George Boss, Fifer.	Hutchins, Jarrett	"
Andrews, John Private.	Hauptman, Daniel	"
Abercrombie, James "	Hall, Edward	"
Briscoe, Alexander "	Howard, Jacob	"
Bennett, Joseph "	Hoffman, David	"
Brice, John "	Harris, Samuel H.	"
Birkhead, James "	Higinbottom, Thos.	"
Brown, John "	Hopkinson, Francis	"
Cruse, William O. "	Johns, William P.	"
Clark, Hooper . "	Jenkins, Felix	"
Chonce, John "	Israel, Fielder	"
Compte, Julius "	Jenkins, Samuel	"
Caldwell, John A. "	Kennedy, William	"
Chase, Stephen "	Kennedy, Mordicai	"
Curtis, J. L. "	Kelso, George G.	"

Lansdale, William M.   Private.
Levely, John S.   "
Lyon, Robert, jr.   "
Lamson, Henry   "
Loney, John   "
Lemmon, Robert   "
Lyles, David C.   "
Linvill, James M.   "
Lytle, Thomas   "
Macenbin, Charles C.   "
McAttic, Francis   "
Moale, Randall H.   "
Patridge, Eaton R.   "
Peirce, Levi, jr.   "
Robinson, Samuel   "
Riggs, George W.   "
Ridgely, Isaiah   "
Rich, John   "
Richards, Lewis M.   "

Rich, George   Private.
Ridgely, James   "
Sillman, Thomas D.   "
Spalding, John   "
Scott, Jeremiah   "
Stewart, William S.   "
Singleton, Charles   "
Schley, Jacob   "
Scott, Henry   "
Shaw, William C.   "
Tilyard, James   " .
Taylor, Robert A.   "
Thomas, Oliver H.   "
Wyse, John M,   "
Walsh, James   "
Yeiser, E. F.   "
Negro George, Capt's Servant.
Negro Welton, Lieut's   "
Negro Thomas, do.   "

BALTIMORE UNION ARTILLERY.

John Montgomery, Captain.
John S. Stiles,   1st Lieut.
Joseph R. Brooks,   2d do.
Jonathan Fitch,   2d do.
Jesse Haslup,   1st Ser'gt.
John Riley,   2d do.
George Eaverson,   3d do.
William Sewell,   4th do.
Alexander Boyd,   1st Corp'l.
George Bartol,   2d do.
Wm. H. Fonerdon,   3d do.
Samuel House,   4th do.
Adreon, George   Private
Armstrong, Thomas   " .
Armstrong, John   "
Bowers, Martin   "
Barger, George   "
Barger, John   "
Barnes, John   "
Bartlett, William   "
Burull, Theophilus   "
Brunett, Andrew   "
Burcroft, Ralph   "
Brown, John   "
Cator, John   "
Chalmers, James   "
Chambers, John M.   "
Chilns, Samuel   "
Curlett, James   "

Curlett, Thomas   Private.
Cros-an, John   "
Campbell, Hugh   "
Churchman, Alfred W.   "
Camcham, James   "
Dwyer, William   "
Delcher, George   "
Davidson, James   "
Donning, William   "
Elliot, Joseph B   "
Elliot, John B.   "
Etchberger, John   "
Erwin, John   "
Franciscus, George   "
Farrall, James W.   "
Finn, John W.   "
German, Jonathan   "
Gill, Ezekiel C.   "
Holland, James   "
Howard, David   "
Hewett, William   "
Hill, Arthur   "
Hazletine, David   "
Jones, Joshua   "
Jordan, Frederick   "
Joseph, Manuel   "
Keen, William, jr.   "
Lamb, John   "
Long, Abraham   "

Lowry, Robert	Private.	Sharkey, Michael	Private.
Mamma, Samuel	"	Stewart, Thomas	"
Mills, Ezekiel	"	Shaw, James B,	"
Mills, William P.	"	Stone, Richard	"
Miller, Frederick	"	Smuch, William	"
Mopps, Adam	"	Stansbury, Elijah	"
Nippard, George	"	Towson, Joshua	"
Pollard, Seth	"	Turner, John	"
Penman, John	"	Walter, John	"
Parker, Evan	"	West, William	"
Renshaw, Thomas S	"	West, John	"
Robinson, John	"	Wimmel, George S.	"
Riley, John	"	Wiese, Frederick A.	"
Rowles, John	"	Williams, Thomas	"
Ringrose, John W.	"	Emanuel, officer's servant.	
Rust, Charles	"	John, "	"
Shade, John	"		

BALTIMORE FENCIBLES.

Josh. H. Nicholson, Captain.
Jesse Eichelberger, 1st Lieut.
Andrew Clopper, 2d do.
Levi Clagett, 3d do.
David Patton, { 1st Ser'gt & 2d Lieut.
John Cleunn, 2d Ser'gt.
Samuel Harris, 3d do.
Wm. Douglas, 4th do.
John Ready, { 1st Corp'l. & 3d Ser'gt.
J. A. Wallace, { 2d Corp'l & 4th Ser'gt.
H. Armstrong, { 3d Corp'l & 2d do.
Ralph Smith { 4th Corp'l & 2d do.

Child, Wm { Private and 4th Corp'l.
Claggett, Thos Private.
Danneman, C. H. "
Dorsey, Joshua { do and 5th Corp'l.
Ditfenderffer, Jno. Private.
Douglass, Geo. "
Dalrymple, Geo. "
Eichelberger, Lewis "
Eichelberger, Wm. "
Etting, Saml. "
Fulton, Wm. S. { do. and 6th Corp'l.
Fernandis, Walter Private.
Guildener, Chas. "
Granger, Jas. "

Arthey, Wm. F. Private.
Alexander, Thomas "
Boyd, Andrew "
Bond, Henry "
Beall, John W. "
Berry, Horatio "
Buckler, John C. "
Brice, James E. "
Cohen, Php. I. "
Cohen, Mendus "
Collins, James W. "
Cooper, Wm. S. "
Conkling, Tho. C. "

Graybell, Php. "
Hawkins, Jas. L. "
Hutchins, Thos. "
Hegenbottom, Jno. "
Horner, Francis "
Hurnessey, Tho. "
Hurdis, James "
Hughes, Wm. "
Howard, Brice "
Jones, Edwd. "
Keller, John "
Lawson, Geo. "
Lerew, John "

Lindenberger, Jb.	Private.	Sands, Benjn. N.	Private.
Mauro, Php.	"	Sylvester, Saml.	"
Maccubin, Moses	"	Spicer, Thos.	"
Monroe, Isaac	"	Schwartze, Hry.	"
Morgan, Edwd.	"	Stickney, Hry.	"
Mayer, Charles F.	"	Snyder, Andw.	"
Neale, John G.	"	Shortt, Jno.	"
Pollett, J. B.	"	Turman, Patrick	"
Poor, Jno. F.	do. and 3d Corp'l.	Vance, William	"
		Williams, Geo.	"
Price, Andw.	Private.	Williams, Cumbd. D.	"
Rogers, Thos.	"	Williams, Nathl. F.	"
Righart, Php.	"	Watkins, Thomas	"
Rigden, Jno. E.	"	Yates, Jno.	"

AMERICAN ARTILLERISTS.

Rd B. Magruder,	Captain.	Davis, Jacob G.	Private.
John Bradford,	1st Lieut.	Delmas, Alevis A.	"
David Griffith,	2d do.	Da'e, Daniel	"
S. J. Thompson,	2d do.	Edwards, Samuel	"
W. H. Wustandley,	3d do.	Fowler, William	"
August Boughan,	1st Ser'gt.	Finlay, John	"
Sam'l Cohen, jr.,	2d do.	French, Ebenezer	"
Wm. G. Elderkin,	3d do.	Furgusson, Thomas	"
Wm. Dew,	4th do.	Falkner, Abraham	"
Stephen Lawson,	1st Corp'l.	Golder, Robert	"
John Casey,	2d do.	Grimes, Joseph	"
Mat. P. Mitchell,	3d do	Glenn, James	"
Adam B. Kyle,	4th do.	Green, Thomas	"
John F. Charlton,	Drummer.	Gambrall, John	"
Wm. Moore, Fifer.		Glenn, John W.	"
Allen, Sam'l W.	Private.	Glenn, John, jr.	"
Allen, James	"	Griffith, Mathew	"
Beall, Rd. B.	"	Howell, Wm. jr.	"
Bond, Joshua	"	Hubball, Ebenezer	"
Brice, John jr.	"	Hicks, John	"
Barcklie, Thomas	"	Hess, Joseph	"
Beatley, Wm. jr.	"	Hillen, Solomon	"
Bose, William	"	Hanson, Wm.	"
Bailey, John H.	"	Howell, John B.	"
Bill, Hugh	"	Hands, Wm. G.	"
Cose, Rd. G.	"	Hess, Jesse	"
Cox, Peter	"	Joice, John	"
Caldwell, Jno. R,	"	Jones, Nicholas S.	"
Crawford, Wm. B.	"	Jonas, Jacob	"
Caldwell, James P.	"	Kinkaid, James	"
Cuzeanse, Bernard	"	Kennedy, Dennis	"
Cooch, Zebulon	"	Linvill, John	"
Dickens, John	"	Magruder, Gustavus	"
Daley, Ben. S.	"	McKee, William	"

McKeel, John	Private.	Starr, William	Private.
Miller, George	"	Schaeffer, F. G.	"
Myers, Stephen	"	Sumwalt, Philip	"
McLaughlin, Philip	"	Sprunig, George	"
Mooses, Parker	"	Stansbury, William	"
Newman, Lawson	"	Taylor, Elijah	"
Norwood, Edward	"	Turner, Nathan	"
Nelson, Benjamin	"	Tarmer, James	"
Petit, Augustus	"	Thomas. John W.	"
Perrine, D. M.	"	Town, John	"
Rudolph, Zebulon	"	Waters, Joseph	"
Robinson, Thomas	"	Waters, Joseph G.	"
Riston, George	"	Wollen, Zachariah	"
Robinson, James	"	Wheeler, Jacob	"
Rose, John P.	"	Wallace, Solomon	"
Robertson, George	"	Wright, William	"
Rickstein, George	"	Wiley, Alexander	"
Ridgeley, Thomas	"	Younker, Francis	"
Simmonds, Samuel	"	Young, Peter A.	"
Shaw, Nathan	"	Nicholas Wallace,	servant.
Starr, Hezekiah	"	William Konig,	"
Simmonds, John A.	"		

WASHINGTON ARTILLERY.

John Berry, Captain.		Carson, William	Private.
Benjamin Buck,	1st Lieut.	Conway, Thomas	"
George Herring,	2d do.	Cassard, Gilbert	"
James Beacham,	3d do.	Collins, Cornelius	"
John Hahn,	1st Serg't.	Cook, Anthony L.	"
James Russell,	2d do.	Carman, Jacob	"
Philip Tilyard,	3d do.	Davis, David	"
Wells Cooper,	4th do.	Duval, Marsh M.	"
James Clark,	1st Corp'l.	Devatur, Jacob	"
Basil Duke,	2d do.	Dare, Nathl. C.	"
Henry Hilbert,	3d do.	Erwin, Jerrard	"
John T. Sumwalt,	4th do.	Foy, James	"
Andrew Hunter, Fifer.		Fahnestock, Derrick	"
Henry Lightner. Drummer.		Fahnestock, Peter	"
Atkinson, Angells	Private.	Fry, John	"
Aisquith, Robert C.	"	Fisher, Jacob	"
Anderson, Wm. M.	"	Gray, William	"
Beison, Thos. V.	"	Gray, John	"
Berry, John W.	"	Hussey, George jr.	"
Berry, Benj. F.	"	Hammer, Jacob	"
Brown, John M.	"	Helm, Leonard	"
Bailey, George W.	"	Hilbert, John	"
Brooks, William	"	Konig, Samuel	"
Baxley, George	"	Lowe, Henderson P.	"
Bartling, Daniel	"	Linch, John	"
Cretzer, John	"	Lowman, Emory	"

Landstreet, John	Private.	Simpson, Erasmus	Private.
Mackey, John jr.	"	Stimple, Anthony	"
Moore, John B.	"	Sumwalt, John X.	"
McElligott, Pierce G.	"	Taylor, James	"
McCubbin, John S.	"	Taylor, Thomas	"
McClain, John	"	Taylor, Levin	"
McLeavy, Henry	"	Taylor, Cromwell	"
Miller, George W.	"	Voyce, Thomas	"
Miller, Matthew	"	Winchester, Thos. C.	"
McMackin, William	"	Wareham, George	"
Nagle, Joseph	"	Wells, Thomas W.	"
Noble, Alexander	"	West, Nicholas	"
Pratt, John H.	"	Williams, Lewis	"
Perry, Richard	"	Whetson, David	"
Pennleton, Daniel	"	Watts, John S.	"
Resser, Jacob	"	Wight, Jesse	"
Reggin, James	"	Watts, Ezekiel	"
Sweeting, Benj. B.	"	Wigart, Henry	"
Storey, John	"	Wamaling, John	"
Smith, Nathl. L.	"	Woods, Samuel	"
Sheebe, John	"	Williams, Jonathan	"
Seaton, Henry	"	Wood, John	"
Shutt, George	"	Young, John	"

BALTIMORE INDEPENDENT ARTILLERISTS.

Charles Pennington, Captain.		Duer, Charles	Private.
Thomas Russell,	1st Lieut.	Dinsmore, Samuel	"
Joseph Clemm,	2d do.	Ellery, Eppes	"
Robert S. Moore,	3d do.	Everett, Edward	"
Thomas Vance,	1st Ser'gt.	Ewaldt, J. H.	"
John S. King,	2d do.	Falconer, Jonathan	"
James C. Wilson,	3d do.	Ford, G. W.	"
Thomas M. Locke,	4th do.	Guthrow, Stephen	"
Benjamin Brooks,	5th do.	Goodrick, Eli	"
Peter L. White,	1st Corp'l.	Greer, George	"
Thos. P. Ricand,	2d do.	Gregg, Alexander	"
John Morton,	3d do.	Harwood, Charles	"
Wm. M. Wallace,	4th . do.	Hayne, George	"
Isaac Taylor,	5th do.	Jessop, Charles	"
Black, Samuel	Private.	Kincaid, Wallace	"
Barkman, John	"	Kent, Emanuel, jr.	"
Branson, Joseph	"	Lusby, William	"
Baker, Charles	"	Lambie, James	"
Bond, J. T.	"	McLaughlin, Peter	"
Birkbead, Lenox	"	McCartney, Peter	"
Cobb, G. K.	"	Meeks, William	"
Callander, J. A.	"	Mackin, James	"
Collins, Lee	"	Mayer, Lewis	"
Cook, W. G.	"	McNeal, James	"
Duncan, Joseph	"	Morehead, Henry	"

Nowland, Lambert	Private.	Thompson, David	Private.
Owens, Isaac	"	Towson, O. W.	"
Osborne, H. P.	"	Taylor, Robert	"
Pascault, Francis	"	Teackle, Severn	"
Patillo, Henry H.	"	Wyville, Marmaduke	"
Rutter, Thomas G.	"	Williams, John	"
Raymond, Daniel	"	Wells, W. T.	"
Rust, Samuel	"	Weir, John R.	"
Sinners, E. R.	"	Walsh, John	"
Shane, Dennis	"	Wilson, J. C.	"
Shields, William	"	Wilhelm, P.	"
Stanley, Joseph	"	Winn, S. D.	"
Stewart, George L.	"	White, Thomas	"
Schaeffer, Christian	"	Zigler, Henry	"
Southcomb, Carey	"	Kleinfelter, Michael	"
Schwartz, A. J. B.	"	Charles Maynard,	servant.
Smith, Samuel	"	Carlos Davies,	"
Street, William	"		

EAGLE ARTILLERISTS.

George J. Brown, Captain.		Dougherty, John	Private.
Thomas Cockrill, 1st Lieut.		Delany, William	"
William Mundell, 2d do.		Gardiner, James	"
Benjamin Rouse, Sergeant.		Groom, William	"
Charles Baker,	do.	Grossh, John	"
James Corner,	do.	Graham, Owen	"
Wm. Gilberthorp,	do.	Harris, Samuel	"
David Greaves,	Corporal.	Jones, George	"
John P. Strobel,	do.	Johnson, Wm. H.	"
Joseph Clark,	do.	Jones, John W.	"
Benjamin Arnold	do.	Johns, William	"
Anderson, Nicholas	Private.	Johnson, Robert	"
Boston, Charles	"	Johnson, Archibald	"
Boss, George	"	Lehea, Morris	"
Binyon, Thomas	"	Lorman, William	"
Bond, Lambert	"	Lenox, James	"
Beard, Hugh	"	Leinhart, Henry	"
Classon, John	"	Myers, Solomon.	"
Chapman, Christopher	"	McCluster, Henry	"
Casey, William	"	McKoan, Edward	"
Chambey, Dennis	"	McClain, Charles	"
Champlin, A. P.	"	Moor, Nathaniel	"
Carrol, Mark	"	Millard, J. L.	"
Dorney, Bartholomew	"	McWilliams, M:	"
Duncan, J. W.	"	Musgrove, Wm.	"
Delaware, Thomas	"	McMullin, Wm.	"
Donoho, Barney	"	Matthews, James	"
Dye, William	"	McNeal, James	"
Donnelly, John	"	O'Cornor, Lewis	"
Daley, John	"	Parks, William	"

Pendigrast, Patrick   Private.   Saunders, Alexander   "
Roache, Alexander   "   Tyler, John   "
Reilly, Patrick   "   Tebo, Peter   "
Ross, James   "   Tebo, Peter, jr.   "
Ritchie, William   "   Tall, Anthony   "
Schofield, J. S.   "   Williams, J. S.   "
Sheridan, Thos.   "   Wallace, James   "

FIRST BALTIMORE VOLUNTEER ARTILLERY.

Abraham Pike,	Captain.	Jones, Jonathan J.	Private.
John King,	1st Lieut.	Inloes, James	"
Reuben Ross,	2d do.	Kirkland, A'exander	"
John Keys,	1st Ser'gt.	Keller, George	"
Thos. H. Fairbain,	2d do.	King, Henry	"
Gotleib Hoffman,	3d do.	Kimmel, Michael	"
Samuel Baum,	4th do.	Lebon, Charles	"
Alex. Osborne,	1st Corp'l.	Linsey, Andrew	"
William Sprole,	2d do.	Lindey, Midhael	"
Wm. Keilholtz,	3d do.	Male, Joseph A.	"
Joshua Gibson,	4th do.	McColm, Mathew	"
Altfather, Henry	Private.	Moore, Henry	"
Ash, John	"	Nicholson, Thomas	"
Armitage, Benj.	"	Orme, Archibald E.	"
Bradley, Isaac	"	Owings, John	"
Black, Thomas	"	Phillips, William	"
Bradebaugh, Jacob	"	Richardson, Ezekiel	"
Butler, Richard	"	Robinson, William	"
Benson, John P,	"	Rider, Arthur	"
Bixler, David	"	Robinson, Thomas	"
Elder, Basil S.	"	Rickey, Wm. W.	"
Foss, George, jr.	"	Shaw, Samuel	"
Fisher, John	"	Sampson, Charles	"
Finley, Thomas	"	Schultz, Conrad	"
Fernandis, Samuel	"	Share, Joseph	"
Foss, Jacob	"	Spangler, Isaac	"
Grubb, Michael, jr-	"	Shamburgh, John	"
Gould, James	"	Seig, Peter	"
Greary, William	"	Wallace, Joseph	"
Garland, John B.	"	Wampler, Lewis J.	"
Hughes, George L.	"	White, George	"
Hussy, Asabel	"	Wedge, Simon	"
Hill, George, jr.	"	Winchester, Samuel	"
Hoffman, John	"	Yager, Joseph	"
Irvine, John	"		

STEINER'S ARTILLERY OF FREDERICK.

Henry Steiner, Captain.   John Buckey,   1st Ser'gt.
R. G. McPherson, 1st Lieut.   William Houser, 2d do.
Lewis Green,   2d do.   Geo. Dertzback, 3d do.

18

David Mantz,	4th Ser'gt.	Heffner, Michael	Private.
Jacob Kieffer,	1st Corp'l.	Holler, Henry	"
William Steiner,	2d do.	Holter, Daniel	"
Henry Hauer,	3d do.	Jamieson, John	"
Marcus Y. Graff,	4th do.	Jenkins, William	"
Jacob Fowble,	Musician.	Johnson, William	"
John Stouffer,	"	Jolly, Thomas M.	"
Ambrose, Peter	Private.	Kontz, John	"
Baer, Michael of Jno.	"	McClain, George	"
Barnes, Samuel	"	McFarland, Peter	"
Blackford, Thomas	"	McPherson, William	"
Belt, Lloyd	"	Murdock, Richard H.	"
Breant, Samuel	"	Miller, John	"
Boyd, David	"	Neaff, Abraham	"
Boone, Robert	"	Nixdorff, Henry	"
Burhhartf Daniel	"	Nichols, Adam	"
Cassell, William	"	Pyfer, Philip	"
Dean, Thomas	"	Potts, Philip	"
Dixon, James	"	Rye, Henry	"
Evett, George	"	Schaffner, Jacob	"
Freburger, Peter	"	Salmon, Charles	"
Feagler, Jacob	"	Steiner, Jno. Thomas	"
Goldsborough, Nich.	"	Shellman, Jacob	"
Grahame, Thomas	"	Scott, Thomas	"
Hanshew, Henry	"	Somerville, James	"
Hauer, George	"	Schissler, John	"
Harding, John L.	"	Schriver, Jacob	"

UNITED MARYLAND ARTILLERY.

James Piper, Captain.		Griffith, Anthony	Private.
Henry Pentz,	1st Lieut.	German, Philip	"
Jacob Walsh,	2d do,	Harker, John	"
John Kennedy,	3d do.	Hetzelberger, John	"
William Drake,	1st Ser'gt.	Harding, Stephen	"
Jesse James,	2d do.	Haislip, Humphy B.	"
Benj. Germain,	3d do.	Johnson, Samuel	"
T. DeLoughrey,	4th do.	Hurst, Elijah	"
Isaac Bull,	1st Corp'l.	Kiernan, John	"
Amasa Kirby,	2d do.	Knight, Peregrine	"
William Wells,	3d do.	Moellinger, Jacob	"
Henry Staylor,	4th do.	Murray, Matthew	"
Browning, Leir	Private.	Maynarn, Quincy	"
Bilson, John	"	Neal, James	"
Constable, George P.	"	Peregoy, Caleb	"
Callmus, Levi	"	Pentz, Daniel	"
Clinedienst, John	"	Roche, James	"
Faherty, Bartley	"	Roche, Joseph	"
Folay, Dennis	"	Rosse, George	"
Gorsuch, John	"	Sommers, Michael	"
Grace, John	"	Snyder, John	"
Griffith, Jacob	"	Staylor, John	"

Staylor, William	Private.	Woods, Septha Private.
Staylor, Philip	"	Wickersham, Wm. "
Stout, Jacob	"	Wise, John M. "
Stackers, Solomon	"	Walker, Samuel "
Smith, Charles	"	Samuel Gourd, Servant.
Trexlear, Ignatius	"	

Names of the Field and Staff and Company Officers, Non-Commissioned Officers and Privates of the First Rifle Battalion of Maryland Militia, who served at North Point and Fort McHenry, 12th September, 1814—taken from the Muster Rolls on file in the office of the Third Auditor of the Treasury of the United States.

WILLIAM PINKNEY, *Major.*
*WILLIAM PINKNEY, JR., *Adjutant.*
JAMES W. MITCHELA, *Quarter Master.*
†SAMUEL B. MARTIN, *Surgeon.*
JOSIAH A. SMITH, *Pay Master.*
B. U. CAMPBELL, *Sergeant Major and Adjutant.*
DANIEL METZKER, *Quarter Master Sergeant.*

SHARP SHOOTERS.

Edward Aisquith,	Captain.	Crouch, James	Private.
John G. Young,	1st Lieut.	Chesnut, John	"
William Meeter,	2d do.	Charlton, William	"
Spencer H. Cone,	3d do.	Dukehart, Henry	"
George W. Howard,	1st Serg't.	Dawson, John	"
Elijah Pritchett,	2d do.	Davis, John G.	"
Alex. McKenzie,	3d do.	Davis, Thomas	"
‡John McFarron,	4th do.	Dunning, Samuel	"
George S. Boyle,	1st Corp'l.	Gruver, John	"
John Burk,	2d do.	Hawkins, James	"
John Hulse,	3d do.	Howard, Jacob	"
Thomas Elligood,	4th do.	Howard, John	"
Batchelor, Smith	Private.	Henry, William	"
Bromwell, Jacob	"	Horsey, Morris	"
Brown, Thomas	"	Hazledine, John	"
Bromwell, Henry T	"	Huzza, John	"
Bruff, Benj.	"	Jeffers, James	"
Buell, Albert D.	"	Jones, Edward	"
Clark, William	"	Jones, Richard	"
Clark, Joseph	"	Kernan, Leonard	"
Camp, William	"	Lythe, John	"
Crawford, William	"	Lee, James A.	"
Curry, John	"	Lafavier, Abraham	"
Creagh, James	"	Macgill, Basil	"

*Wounded at Bladensburg.   †Prisoner.   ‡Taken off the field by Surgeon Worter.

*McComas, Henry	Private.	Parrish, William	Private
Martin, James E.	"	Rusk, Thomas	"
Macgill, Thomas	"	Rumsey, Charles H.	"
Melliss, William	"	Small, Jacob T.	"
Mitchell, Alexander	"	Stewart, John	"
Murray, John E.	"	Watts, Dixon B.	"
Noble, Richard	"	Watts, Thomas B.	"
Prettyman, Thomas G.	"	Watson, Sylvester	"
Prettyman, David G.	"	*Wells, Daniel	"
Pettygrew, James	"	Warner, John	"

UNION YAGERS.

Dominic Bader, Captain.		Hetzler, John	Private.
*Gregorious Andre, 1st Lieut.		Hoffman, Lawrence	"
B. U. Campbell,	1st do.	Jacobs, John	"
Jos. A. Strischka,	2d do.	James, Charles	"
Caspar Hoffman, Ensign.		Jorden, John	"
†Jacob Euler,	1st Ser'gt.	Johanness, William B.	"
John M. Metler!	2d do.	Kummer, Frederick	"
Wm. Ebervine,	3d do.	Keipple, Henry	"
John Small,	4th do.	Koellenger, Henry	"
Martin Hirsch,	1st Corp'l.	Leatherwood, John	"
John Gieger,	2d do.	Long, Francis	"
J. L. Koellinger,	3d do.	Moses, Jacob	"
James Fisher,	4th do.	Miller, Philip	"
Adam Wilhelm, Bugler.		Meyer, John	"
Armeger, Benjamin	Private.	Meyer, Adam	"
Armstrong, John	"	Meads, Daniel	"
Banier, Frederick	"	Metz, Peter	"
Baker, Peter	"	Renner, John	"
Barkman, Conrad	"	Roab, J. P.	"
Brown, John	"	Rothe, William	"
Crane, Joseph	"	Rehberg, J. L.	"
Disney, Wesley	"	Rothemond, Dietrick	"
Disney, James	"	Schultz, John	"
DeGoy, Bartholomew	"	Schaub, Jacob	"
Dawson, William	"	Scharffer, William	"
Darnes, Augustus	"	Steinforth, John	"
Durst, Felix J.	"	Schronder, Henry	"
Euler, Conrad	"	Steidel, Gotleib	"
Franklin, George	"	Turner, David G.	"
Fowble, William	"	Undrech, Henry	"
Fisher, John	"	Van Harten, Gerrard	"
Fisher, Abraham	"	Wulpy, William	"
Frederick, Lawrence	"	Wiegant, Daniel	"
Fogleman, George	"	Walter, Henry	"
Gusenderffer, John	"	Weddekin, John	"
Grub, Michael	"		

*Killed. †Wounded.

FELL'S POINT RIFLEMEN.

William B. Dyer,	Captain.	Gravy, William	Private.
Peter Foy,	1st Lieut.	Hagthorp, Thomas	"
Ephraim Smith,	2d do.	Hall, Henry	"
Thomas D. Rook,	3d do.	Harris, Nehemia	"
John Gorsuch,	Ensign.	Harrison, Charles	"
Daniel Metzger,	1st Ser'gt.	Harding, Christopher	"
F. Monmonier,	2d do.	Hanson, Benedict H.	"
Abraham Parks,	3d do.	Hawkins, Daniel	"
Thomas Mitchell,	4th do.	Jones, James	"
Elijah Dyer.	1st Corp'l.	James, Robert	"
Daniel Anthony,	2d do.	Lock, Samuel	"
Thomas Hall,	3d do.	Lock, William	"
John Johnson,	4th do.	March, Gale	"
Agnew, William	Private.	Maddox, Richard	"
Austin, Benjamin,	"	McDonald, James	"
Ardrery, John E.	"	McAllister, Richard	"
Allen, Samuel	"	McGenerty, Patrick	"
Ashcroft, Thomas	"	Marselas, John E.	"
Bishop, Richard	"	Marselas, James	"
Blades, Benjamin	"	Nicoll, Thomas	"
Burman, Henry	"	Parsons, Jonathan	"
Blades, Perry	"	Pilchard, William	"
Bishop, Richard R.	"	Polk, Cordo	"
Bowen, Richard	"	Ramsay, Joseph	"
Bryson, James	"	Richards, Benedict	"
Clark, John	"	Riggen, James	"
Carter, Thomas	"	Robertson, John	"
Cully, Robert	"	Rouse, James	"
Collins, Isaac	"	Sweeting, Joshua	"
Cormacul, John	"	Sherwood, Philip	"
Dawson, Joseph	"	Speck, Henry	"
Davy, William	"	Shreck, William	"
Dummond, Richard	"	Stinchcomb, Aquilla	"
Dyer, Ezekiel	"	Vanwinkle, William	"
Denny, Joseph	"	Vanwinkle, Samuel	"
*Earnest, Charles	"	Wilson, Joseph	"
Evans, Elias	"	West, William	"
Foble, Daniel	"	Watts, Edward	"
Gordon John	"	Walker, Jonathan	"
Gordon, Richard	"	Wright, John	"

*Wounded.

Names of the Officers, Non-Commissioned Officers, Musicans and Privates of Capt. George Stiles' Corps of Marine Artillery, who served at North Point and Fort McHenry, 12th September, 1814:

MARINE ARTILLERY.

George Stiles,	Captain.	Durand, John	Private.
Joseph Gould,	1st Lieut.	Duncan, Perry	"
Baptist Mezick,	1st do.	Despaux, Elie	"
Timothy Gardner,	2d do.	Darrell, Sampson	"
Joel Vickers,	2d do.	Demsford, John	"
Francis Blackwell,	3d do.	Despaux, John	"
John G. Bier,	Qr. Master.	Deale, James	"
Benjamin Weeks,	Sergeant.	Ellis, George	"
David Chaytor,	"	Frazier, James	"
Paul Durkee,	"	Furlong, William	"
William Spear,	"	Franklin, Benjamin	"
Edward Wynne,	"	Garretson, R. W.	"
Egbert Van Buren,	"	Gilbert, George	"
John Raynolds,	Drummer.	Gregg, A. P.	"
John Miller,	Fifer.	Goxdwait, E.	"
Allen, Holden	Private.	Gavet, John	"
Baker, Rathbone	"	Gardner, W. H.	"
Bennett, Thomas B.	"	Guarnego, Louis	"
Bennett, Field F.	"	Grant, Henry	"
Barrar, John, jr.	"	Gardner, Samuel	"
Bolten, Henry	"	Gorden, Walton	"
Barnes, W. P.	"	Glenn, R. W.	"
Belt, Tobias J.	"	Hollis, W. C.	"
Brennan, John F.	"	Hyland, John	"
Brotherton, William	"	Hutson, John	"
Belt, James, jr.	"	Hamilton, Pliny	"
Beam, George, jr.	"	Hall, John	"
Bargan, Joseph	"	Hearth, J. T.	"
Braggen, Henry	"	Hammell, Samuel	"
Bilup, Robert	"	Hill, John	"
Bowie, James	"	Holmes, James	"
Cunningham, John	"	Hillert, John A.	"
Cordery, James	"	Hughs, James	"
Crane, John	"	Hancock, Robert	"
Curtis, James	"	Habrkiss, S. H.	"
Clackner, Joseph	"	Hayes, W. C.	"
Coleman, Christopher	"	Johnson, James	"
Cathel, William	"	Jenks, T. W.	"
Cock, John	"	Jacobs, Wilson	"
Dawson, Joseph	"	James, Daniel	"
Dickinson, P.	"	Jackson, Thadeus	"
Davis, Robert	"	Kirk, George	"
Denny, Richard A.	"	Kinnard, Thomas	"
Dashiel, Henry	"	Kelly, Matthew	"

Lane, Thomas M.	Private.	Ratier, Thomas	Private.
Lee, George	"	Rhodes, Zachariah	"
Laty, John	"	Ross, John	"
Myers, N.	"	Riddle, Edward	"
McMeal, Daniel	"	Smith, B. B.	"
Mills, George	"	Southcomb, P.	"
Morrison, John	"	Scott, John	"
Mezick, Joshua	"	Shipley, Samuel	"
Monsarrat, D.	"	Shaw, Daniel	"
McElderry, Hugh	"	Stevens, James H.	"
Manadier, D.	"	Smith, John S.	"
McClaskey, A.	"	Southwait, William	"
Morris, T. C.	"	Snow, Freeman	"
McCombs, Solo	"	Tucker, W. A.	"
Neighle, Francis	"	Tilden, Perry	"
Ninde, Isaac	"	Thomas, William	"
Orrick, John	"	Thompson, John	"
Owen, William	"	Thomas, Joseph	"
Perry, Charles G.	"	Vicker, James	"
Peterson, John	"	Weve, James	"
Peterkin, William	"	Wilkinson, S.	"
Philips, James	"	Wilson, David	"
Parrott, David	"	White, John M.	"
Patterson, Gerard	"	Weems, George	"
Prior, John	"	Williams, William R.	"
Peterson, John, jr.	"	Wade, William	"
Russell, Samuel	"	Watkins, James	"
Ramsay, James	"	Young, John	"
Reppard, Jacob	"	Young, William	"
Rozen, Jacob	"	Henderson, Robert	"
Rollins, James	"		

YORK VOLUNTEERS,

ATTACHED TO THE FIFTH REGIMENT MARYLAND VOLUNTEER INFANTRY.

Michl. H. Spangler, Captain.		Coil, Daniel	Private.
Jacob Barnitz, jr., 1st Lieut.		Duvall, Grafton	"
John Kuntz, 2d Ser'gt.		Dunn, George	"
Joseph Schall,	"	Devine, John	"
David Wilson, Corporal.		Dugan, James	"
Daniel Updegraff,	"	Frey, Jacob	"
Michl. Hahn,	"	Fisher, John	"
Adam Leitner, Musician.		Glessner, Jacob	"
Altemus, Jerman W.	Private.	Grimes, Peter	"
Burns, Anthony T.	"	Gartner, Jacob	"
Brigle, George	"	Holton, George	"
Burns, John	"	Hoffart, David	"
Connelly, James	"	Hoit, Aaron	"

Ingram, Hugh	Private.	Noel, Jacob	Private.
Ilgenfritz, George	"	Reisinger, Jacob	"
Kaufman, David	"	Rauss, Emanuel	"
Kaufman, Andrew	"	Rupp, Jacob	"
Lottman, Jacob	"	Stuck, Charles	"
Lehman, Jacob	"	Sinn, John	"
Lavan, Jacob	"	Schleiger, Henry	"
Leitner, George M.	"	Stoeling, Jacob	"
Lanius, Peter	"	Sheffer, Jacob	"
Leitner, Joseph	"	Smith, Chester	"
Laub, George	"	Thompson, Thomas	"
McClean, John	"	Thompson, Enoch	"
Miller, Michael	"	Taylor, John	"
Mundorff, Henry	"	Trimble, David	"
McKonigher, Joseph	"	Wisenhall, Jacob	"
Nes, William	"	Witz, Frederick	"
Nes, Samuel	"		

HANOVER VOLUNTEERS,

ATTACHED TO THE THIRTY-NINTH REGIMENT MARYLAND MILITIA.

Frederick Metzger, Captain.		Hines, Samuel	Private.
Henry Wirt, 1st Lieut.		Hilt, Jacob	"
George Immel, 2d do.		Hostetter, Jacob	"
George Eiler, Ensign.		Horn, Jesse	"
David Shultz,	1st Ser'gt.	Haas, Christian	"
Benjamin Welsh,	2d do.	Hawks, Samuel	"
George Stanter,	3d do.	Hoffman, William	"
Henry Melsheimer,	4th do.	Jarvis, Thomas	"
John Rieder,	1st Cor'pl.	Koon, Solomon	"
Joseph Morris,	2d do.	Klein, Henry	"
Daniel Little,	3d do.	Myers, John	"
George Hoke,	4th do.	Morningstar, George	"
Apple, Philip	Private.	Melshamer, William	"
Bargelt, John	"	Myers, George	"
Beck, Tobias	"	Michael, John	"
Buvinger, Leonard	"	Richards, Edward	"
Bange, John	"	Storm, David	"
Bange, Henry	"	Short, Anthony	"
Blinzinger, David	"	Stock, Henry	"
Cramer, Jacob	"	Stoehr, Daniel	"
Dines, John	"	Waggoner, Jacob	"
Douglass, John	"	Weigle, John	"

HAGERSTOWN VOLUNTEERS,

ATTACHED TO THE THIRTY-NINTH REGIMENT MARYLAND MILITIA.

Thomas Quantrill, Captain.	Kinkerly, Jacob	Private.
Daniel Sprigg, 1st Lieut.	Knease, Frederick	"
George Harry, 2d do.	Lynes, George	"
William Shall, Ensign.	Loney, Jacob	"
Thomas Keen, 1st Ser'gt.	Locker, Jacob	"
Wm. McCardell, 2d do.	McPherrin, William	"
George Kreps, 3d do.	McDonough, John	"
John Harry, 4th do.	Man, Solomon	"
John Hunter, 1st Corp'l.	Miller, John N.	"
Daniel Oyster, 2d do.	Morter, Jacob	"
Benjamin Smith, 3d do.	Martiney, John	"
Joseph Cellers, 4th do.	McClanahan, Robert	"
Charles Duwasser, Musician.	Martin, Anthony B.	"
Anderson, John Private.	Neal, Joseph	"
Allison, William "	Noble, James	"
Armour, William "	O'Ferrall, John	"
Bayley, Samuel "	Patton, Columbus	"
Bechart, Jacob "	Poffenbarger, Andrew	"
Billenger, John "	Shnebly, John	"
Bennet, Samuel "	Soper, Thomas	"
Barnes, Samuel W. "	Stroud, Joseph	"
Couley, John "	Shank, Samuel	"
Cramer, John "	Smith, Daniel	"
Collins, Andrew "	Shipley, John	"
Coke, Alexander "	Schleigh, William	"
Cook, John T. "	Sterret, James	"
Deitz, John "	Schryock, David	"
Daup, Daniel "	Smith, Peter	"
Glassbremmer, Peter "	Snecdor, John	"
Goyer, Jacob "	Smith, John	"
Harry, William "	Srit, John	"
Hemphill, Joseph "	Wagman, John	"
Helser, Philip "	Wilson, Lazarus	"
Humrickhouse, Fred'k. "	Wilson, Samuel	"
Harry, Samuel "	Wareham, Joseph	"
Hawkin, Daniel "	West, Levin	"
Johnston, John "	Winters, George	"
Kealy, Jacob "	Wise, George	"
Keallyer, Jesse "		

MARYLAND CAVALRY.

Jacob Baer, Captain.
David Newcomer, 1st Lieut.
Samuel Bohrer, 2d do.
Henry Kilhofer, Cornet.
Jacob Hughett, Sergeant.
Benjamin Kershner, "
Otto Adams, "
Jacob Kershner, "
Samuel Alter, Corporal.
Levey Rensh, "
Frederick Rohrer, "
John Walkernoot, "
Adams, Jacob   Private.
Adams, Williams,   "
Anderson, William   "
Winders, John   "
Binkley, Jacob   "
Miller, John   "
Miller, Henry   "
Dillibunt, James   "
Knode, Jacob   "
Witmore, John   "
Yeakel, Jacob   "

Repp, John   Private.
Willson, Edward H.   "
Kindell, Joseph   "
Cellers, John   "
Fabbs, Moses   "
Krider, George   "
Kline, Daniel   "
Gurlaugh, Henry   "
Berry, James   "
Degraft, Abraham   "
Waller, Henry   "
Kitz, Frederick   "
Miller, Daniel   "
Thomas, George   "
Clagett, David   "
Goll, John   "
Howard, John   "
Kershner, George   "
Wayman, Perry   "
Philip Binkley, Q. M. Ser'gt.
John Kailhofer, Saddler.
Jacob Leider, Blacksmith.
Joseph Eakel, Trumpeter.

Names of the Field and Staff and Company Officers, Non-Commissioned Officers and Privates of the fifth Regiment of Infantry of the Maryland Militia, who served at North Point and Fort McHenry, 12th September, 1814—taken from the Muster Rolls on file in the office of the Third Auditor of the Treasury of the United States:

JOSEPH STERRETT, *Lieutenant Colonel Commandant.*
RICHARD K. HEATH, 1st *Major.*
STANDISH BARRY, 2d do.
JAMES CHESTON, *Lieutenant and Adjutant.*
JOHN OWEN, *Surgeon.*
JOHN THOMAS, *Lieutenant and Quarter Master.*
ALEXANDER H. BOYD, *Lieutenant and Pay Master.*
JOHN B. TAYLOR, *Surgeon's Mate.*
WILLIAM DIFFENDEFFER, *Sergeant Major.*
JOHN L. POTTS, *Quarter Master Sergeant.*

BALTIMORE YEAGERS.

Philip B. Sadtler,	Captain.	Kuhn, A. C.	Private.
C. Newhaus,	1st Lieut.	Keeney, A.	"
T. C. Proetsting,	2d do.	Laudun, M.	"
J. C. Wagner,	1st Ser'gt.	Lash, Geo.	"
F. W. Henke,	2d do.	Markert, Augst.	"
N. Hacke,	3d do.	Meyer, G.	"
Js. Klee,	4th do.	Meyer, A.	"
A. Duluc,	1st Corp'l.	Mozer, J. D.	"
B. Roesehen,	2d do.	McKey, M.	"
J. C. Rau,	3d do.	Muth, P.	"
App, J. S.	Private.	Opperman, L.	"
Brenning, C.	"	Pontier, J.	"
Buhring, F.	"	Parlette, Mordecai	"
Bowers, George	"	Roesener, J.	"
Cassary, Jacob	"	Rodemeyer, G.	"
Crey, Frederick	"	Rogge, Chs.	"
Descande, And.	"	Riep, Henry	"
Deroncery, Chs.	"	Reune, Peter	"
Dail, Chs.	"	Schminke, Geor.	"
Dover, H.	"	Schwier, Jos.	"
Fave, Jo.	"	Sauerwein, Peter	"
Fahs, Casper	"	Sanderson, H.	"
Flowers, B.	"	Schneckpepper, J. B.	"
Gehring, Ge.	"	Singer, George	"
Gilbach, Chs.	"	Schutt, A.	"
Hoffman, H.	"	Steinbock, J. C.	"
Hasselman, L.	"	Smith, N.	"
Hammer, A.	"	Saltzwedel, J.	"
Hauds, P. G.	"	Spicknall, W.	"
Hitzelberger, Js.	"	Taylor, Jos.	"
Janes, E.	"	Walter, T.	"
Klockengetter, Dl.	"	West, J.	"
Klassen, C.	"	Wilson, J.	"
Knodt, A.	"	Wills, F. M.	"
Knodt, J.	"	Wheeler, R. W.	"
Kaylar, Geo.	"		

FIRST BALTIMORE LIGHT INFANTRY.

John Shrim, Captain.		Joseph Pearson,	1st Corp'l.
Nicholas Elliott, Lieutenant.		Mordecai Disney,	do.
John Weaver, Ensign.		Wm. Booth,	do.
John Simonson,	1st Ser'gt.	James Barker,	do.
Andrew Hoffman,	2d do.	Adams, Benjn.	Private.
Joseph Russell,	3d do.	Andrews, George	"
John Hoburg,	4th do.	Auld, John	"

Bidison, Abraham	Private.	Hopkins, Joshua	Private.
Ball, Walter	"	Harman, John	"
Bell, William	"	Horze, William	"
Buckingham, Levi	"	Hass, William	"
Bell, James	"	Henning, George	"
Booth, Joseph	"	Hoburg, Harman	"
Barnes, William	"	Hanson, Henry	"
Cook, George	"	Haney, Charles	"
Cross, John	"	Keener, William	"
Carnighan, James	"	Leeson, John	"
Carson, John	"	Lucas, Joseph	"
Cathrall, Joseph	"	Lacount, Thomas	"
Connelly, Thomas	"	Mowbary, Henry	"
Dobbins, William	"	Mosher, William	"
Davidson, Robert	"	Miller, Charles	"
Dunn, John	"	Matthews, Elias	"
Disney, William	"	Nelson, Joseph, jr.	"
Demuth, John	"	Peters, Daniel	"
Davis, John	"	Popp, Chas. F.	"
Devone, Frederick	"	Pindell, John	"
Davidson, Samuel	"	Rothrock, Philip	"
Deets, Gottleib	"	Ready, Joseph	"
Essender, John	"	Rudenstein, John M.	"
Fyia, John	"	Snyder, Valentine	"
Fonder, Peter	"	Smithson, Daniel	"
Foreman, Christian	"	Stewart, John	"
Franciscus, Wm.	"	Shane, Daniel	"
Foreman, Valentine	"	Suter, Henry	"
Freyer, Henry	"	Thomas, Lambert	"
Freyburger, George	"	Wyneman, John B.	"
Forrester, Ralph E.	"	Welshoover, Henry	"
Gardner, George	"	Wolf, Michael	"
Granger, Samuel	"	Wetherstand, Jacob	"
Grubb, George	"	Workinger, Jacob	"
Glover, William	"	West, Saml. H.	"
Groves, Isaac	"	White, Nicholas	"
Greenfield, John	"	Zigler, Jacob	"
Hinds, William	"		

MECHANICAL VOLUNTEERS.

Benj. C. Howard, Captain.
Thomas Towson, Lieutenant.
Joseph Cox, Ensign.
George Mathiot, Ser'gt.
James Stewart, do.
John Bull, do.
George Hull, do.
John Yewell, Corp'l.
Joseph Thomas, do.

Francis Castine, Corp'l.
Joseph Whittaker, Musician.
George Whittaker, "
Adie, Edmond Private.
Anderson, John "
Baughman, Frederick "
Balderson, Isaiah "
Barc, George "
Bainer, William "

Bell, Thomas	Private.	Peters, Haury C.	Private.
Boren, George	"	Poque, Lowdie J.	"
Biven, Horatio	"	Randall, Aquila	"
Canby, Benjn.	"	Randall, Elisha	"
Collins, Joseph	"	Redgrave, John	"
Dudley, George	"	Reezer, Saml. C.	"
Dulaney, Samuel	"	Ritazel, Francis	"
Dalrymple, Wm.	"	Rote, John	"
Hayden, Dennis	"	Shaw, Isaiah	"
Hitzelberger, Anthony	"	Sifton, Wm.	"
Hoopman, John	"	Sinclair, James	"
Hutton, Elisha	"	Stansbury, Darius	"
Hoar, Elias	"	Stockton, John	"
Hull, Edward	"	Simpers, Benjn.	"
Jones, Joshua	"	Sindall, John	"
Kimes, Thomas	"	Towson, Henry H.	"
Levy, Thomas	"	Turner, Charles	
Mathiot, Christian	"	Tyler, John C.	
Marser, Bartholomew	"	Willing, Josiah	
Meyer, Jacob	"	Wells, Harrison	"
Mills, Levin	"	Yanaway, Daniel	"

WASHINGTON BLUES.

George H. Stewart, Captain.		Gould, Alexr.	Private.
Francis Forster, Lieutenant.		Hill, Thomas	"
Campbell S. Askew, Ensign.		Holland, Joseph	"
Edwd. J. Coale,	1st Ser'gt.	Harrison, Benjn.	"
Thomas Neilson,	2d do.	Hunt, Jesse	"
Richardson Galt,	3d do.	Janvier, Peregrine	"
John M. Howland,	4th do.	Jenkins, Michael	"
Wm. Spurier,	1st Corp'l.	Jenkins, Charles	"
Wm Bradford,	2d do.	Jenkins, George	"
Thomas Ruckle,	3d do.	Kimberly, Nathl.	"
John R. Kelso,	4th do.	Lamb, George	"
Augustine, Samuel	Private.	Long, Jesse	"
Bassett, Isaac	"	Lockhead, Joseph	"
Brandt, Jacob	"	Lynch, William	"
Buchanan, Lloyd	"	Mallonee, John	"
Burke, Jacob	"	Munroe, Alvin	"
Cooksey, Richd. K.	"	Norris, Edward	"
Coulter, John P.	"	Orchard, John	"
Cramer, Geo. W.	"	Pearson, Elias	"
Croxall, James	"	Pollitt, Wm. F.	
Dougherty, John	"	Ruckle, Samuel	"
Dougherty, James	"	Schryake, William	"
Faulac, Anthony	"	Stewart, Wm. P.	"
Flaherty, John R.	"	Spurier, Beale	

Shutt, John P.	Private.	Waters, Asa	Private.
Symington, Jas. F.	"	Waters, Peter	"
Stevens, Peter	"	Waters, Zebulon	"
Tharpe, George	"	Wright, Malcolm	"
Usher, James	"	Wilson, William	"
Vanlear, John	"	Webb, James	"
Wall, John E.	"		

INDEPENDENT COMPANY.

Samuel Sterrett, Captain.		Larsh, Abrm.	Private.
John Hillen, Lieutenant.		Lucas, Sam.	"
John Reese, Ensign.		McFaden, J. jr.	"
Chrisr. Raborg, 1st Ser'gt.		McDowell, G.	"
Ben. D. Higdon, 2d do.		McKenzie, G.	"
H. P. Sumner, 3d do.		Mackall, E.	"
Michl. Sanderson, 4th do.		Murray, Edwd.	"
John Frick, 1st Corporal.		Martracy, J.	"
Alexander, H.	Private.	Martin, John	"
Armstrong, T.	"	McDonald, P.	"
Brice, Nicholas	"	McDonald, H.	"
Baker, Tho. B.	"	Norris, William	"
Bailey, Thomas	"	Norris, Thomas	"
Burt, And.	"	Owens, Joseph	"
Baker, Wm. jr.	"	Patrick, L. C.	"
Birckhead, H.	"	Purviance, James	"
Baine, Hope	"	Porter, William	"
Camp, William	"	Porter, Michl.	"
Caldwell, James	"	Patterson, Jno.	"
Coleman, John	"	Rogers, Wm.	"
Dewees, And.	"	Rogers, Geo.	"
Darrington, W.	"	Rogers, Daniel	"
Devenie, James	"	Stump, Sam.	"
Fulford, Henry	"	Small, John	"
Fimister, Alexr.	"	Seyler, Fred.	"
Goodwyn, C. D.	"	Shock, Henry	"
Graff, F. C.	"	Trull, John	"
Gitchell, J.	"	Tanner, P. S.	"
Hollingsworth, L.	"	Uhler, Philip	"
Harden, Saml.	"	Waters, Jno. S.	"
Hughes, John	"	Wilson, William	"
Hindes, M.	"	Warner, Wm.	"
Herbert, John	"	Williams, Nat.	"
Hughes, Dens.	"	Wall, William	"
Jenkins, Edwd.	"	White, Gideon	"
Jones, Talbot	"	Wheeden, H.	"
Jones, R. H.	"	Williams, A. A.	"
Levering, John	"	Watson, Robt.	"
Levering, Jesse	"		

BALTIMORE UNITED VOLUNTEERS.

David Warfield, Captain.	Golder, George	Private.
William Cooke, Lieutenant.	Gray, Henry W.	"
John Wilmot, Ensign.	Greetham, Wm.	"
Nicholas Dubois, 2d Ser'gt.	Gwinn, Edward	"
George Sears, 3d "	Grundy, Thomas B.	"
Wm. H. Murray, 4th "	Hays, Reverdy	"
John M. Finley, 1st Corp'l.	Haubert, Jacob	"
Joseph Baker, 2d do.	Hearsey, Geo. T.	"
Joseph Barling, 3d do.	Hamilton, Wm.	"
J. W. McCulloch, 4th do.	Holland, R. W.	"
John McHenry, 5th Ser'gt.	Hollingsworth, Horatio	"
W. B. Atterbury, 6th do.	Howard, Henry	"
Wm. B. Bend, 5th Corp'l.	Irwin, John	"
George Cooke, 6th do.	Jackson, John E.	"
Aldridge, Andrew Private.	Jenkins, Frederick	"
Anderson, A. M. "	Jones, T. A.	"
Alexander, Jos. "	Keerl, John C.	"
Adgate, Andrew "	Keerl, Samuel	"
Armands, James "	Keener, Christian, jr.	"
Adams, George "	Kennedy, John P. jr.	"
Armour, David "	Lemmonier, A. L.	"
Bankson, John "	McCubbin, Wm. H.	"
Baker, Geo. J. "	McClellan, William	"
Baker, John "	Merryman, John, jr.	"
Baynard, John "	Mauldin, John	"
Beatty, Henry "	Meredith, Jonathan	"
Biscoe, Walter "	Miller, Robt. jr.	"
Blair, William "	Monk, George	"
Bruff, William "	Mulliken, Rignal	"
Byrd, John C. "	Morehead, Turner	"
Brice, Henry "	Muschett, Walter	"
Bunbury, H. A. "	Mullikin, Barruck	"
Caustin, Jas. H. "	Montgomery, James	"
Chaffee, Natham M. "	Marsh, Dennis	"
Clagett, Elie "	Magruder, Dennis F.	"
Clarke, Geo. W. "	Nelson, Oliver H.	"
Cochran, Wm. G. "	O'Rourke, Charles	"
Courtnay, Wm. "	Owen, R. H.	"
Dunbar, Geo. T. "	Perkins, John	"
Dawes, Jas. G. "	Philips, Isaac, jr.	"
Delacour, James "	Pike, Henry	"
Easterbrook, David "	Poor, John H.	"
Emory, Thos. L. "	Pochon, Chas.	"
Fahnestock, Henry "	Pogue, John G.	"
Flanagan, John R. "	Proud, Wm. T.	"
Freeland, Egbert "	Pringle, Mark W.	"
Frelett, Augustus "	Priestly, Edward	"
Gilmor, William "	Purviance, Robert	"
Gibson, James "	Pennington, Josias	"

Pogue, James, jr.	Private.	Sewell, John M.	Private.
Purse, James	"	Stone, James, jr.	"
Pierce, William	"	Torrence, George	"
Ratcliffe, Luther	"	Taylor, Benjamin	"
Rennell, John N.	"	Van Wyck, Stedman R.	"
Reinicker, Henry	"	Wellford, R. T.	"
Ridgely, Edward	"	Wood, John	"
Roberts, John	"	Wilson, Robert	"
Rutter, John	"	Wells, Cyprian F.	"
Swann, John E.	"	Walker, Thomas	"
Snowden, Joseph	"	Williams, William	"
Swann, William	"	Williams, Isaac	"
Starke, George	"	Werdebaugh, John	"
Smith, Job, jr.	"	Young, Wm. L.	"
Schroeder, Edward	"		

UNION VOLUNTEERS.

Christian Adreon, Captain.		Jordon, James	Private.
Saml. John Lee, Lieutenant.		Kelly, Perry	"
Hy. W. Dettman, Ensign.		Lambert, Lewis	"
William Fish, 1st Ser'gt.		Lawton, Jacob H.	"
James Merriken, 2d do.		Marriott, Jas. H.	"
Elisha Marriott, 3d do.		McCarter, James	"
Joshua Dryden, 1st Corp'l.		McElwee, Samuel	"
Jacob Medairy, 2d do.		McCubbin, Moses	"
Wm. Jarvis, 3d do.		Merriken, Jacob	"
Alexander, Robert	Private.	McKesseck, John	"
Armor, John	"	Medairy, John	"
Bennett, George	"	McMullin, Timothy	"
Brandon, Charles	"	Nicholson, Josa H.	"
Barnett, Joseph	"	Oldson, Samuel	"
Culbert, Lewin	"	Putsar, Martin	"
Cross, Christian A.	"	Pidgeon, John	"
Clemmins, John	"	Patterson, Thomas	"
Collins, Geo.	"	Parker, Charles	"
Cook, Caleb	"	Polkinghorn, Richard	"
Cook, John F.	"	Shaw, Samuel	"
Davis, William	"	Smith, John	"
Dugan, George	"	Smith, Thomas	"
Davis, David	"	Thiel, Jeremiah	"
Evans, George	"	Tittle, Jeremiah	"
Green, Samuel	"	Tittle, Samuel	"
Hook, Michael	"	Timanus, John	"
Hadaway, James	"	Toy, John D.	"
Hildebrandt, Andrew	"	Thornton, Joseph	"
Hildebrandt, Christian	"	Warren, Daniel	"
Hayes, John	"	Wilson, Robert	"
Hagner, George	"	Wyant, George John	"

Wysham, Thomas	Private.	Walter, John	Private.
White, Peter	"	Young, Jacob	"
Working, Frederick	"	Zimmerman, Hy. H.

BALTIMORE PATRIOTS.

Robert Lawson, Captain.	Gregg, James	Private.
Samuel Hutton, 1st Lieut.	Grieves, John	"
John Sinclair, Ensign.	Johnson, Thomas	"
John Hoey,	Sergeant.	Kelser, Wm.	"
Richard Barnett,	. do.	Kelly, James	"
Samuel Harris,	do.	Lynch, James	"
David K. Richardson, Corp'l.	Meredith, Benjn.	"
James Gantt,	do.	Morehead, John	"
Wm. Howell,	do.	McCoul, Robert	"
Arsters, Alexr.	Private.	McCoul, James	"
Deal, John	"	McGuchin, Alexr.	"
Ford, John	"	Oldson, Saml.	"
Fenning, Dennis	"	Poe, David	"
Grezell, Francis	"	Reynolds, Richard	"
Graham, David	"	Stilts, William	"
Gifford, Alexr.	"	Tucker, Joshua	"
Garvin, Thomas	"

INDEPENDENT BLUES.

Aaron R. Levering, Captain.	Bohn, Charles, jr.	Private.
John Bradenbaugh, Lieut.	Brosius, Michael	"
William Wilson, jr. Ensign.	Bickford, James	"
Samuel Myers,	Serg't.	Baker, John	"
Joseph Sumeralt,	"	Barry, Thomas	"
Daniel Kruler,	"	Cole, Samuel	"
George Myers,	"	Clemm, William	"
Charles Dorsey,	Corp'l.	Chappell, Wm. L.	"
John G. Chappell,	"	Causter, Wm. C.	"
Geo. S. Eichelberger,	"	Croxall, Richard	"
Armstrong, John	Private.	Crook, Charles, jr.	"
Alcock, William, jr.	"	Cole, John	"
Albert, Jacob	"	Chaffer, Amos	"
Bride, Henry	"	Deloste, Francis	"
Boyer, Jacob	"	Davidson, Samuel	"
Bare, Samuel	"	Decker, Jacob F.	"
Belt, Thomas W.	"	Deffendoffer, Charles	"
Berteau, F. C.	"	Duboise, James	"
Barry, John	"	Eulon, Philip	"
Ball, John	"	Elliott, George	"

Eichelberger, George	Private.	Norris, Acquilla	Private.
Emory, Gideon	"	Norris, Silas C.	"
Eccleston, James	"	Owens, William	"
Eichelberger, William	"	Parker, James	"
Fulton, James	"	Phoenix, Thomas	"
Foltz, William	"	Pence, Joseph	"
Fairburn, James	"	Piat, John	"
Griffeth, Howard	"	Powder, George	"
Gregg, Andrew	"	Pogen, John	"
Grandshamp, Wm.	"	Price, Nichodemus	"
Gwinn, Benjamin	"	Rusk, William	"
Gallagher, Leslie	"	Ross, Benj. C.	"
Gover, Philip	"	Rogers, Richard	"
Fetz, Frederick	"	Richardson, Daniel	"
Heidelbaugh, George	"	Rogers, Elisha	"
Hutchins, James	"	Robinson, Benj. H.	"
Hall, Richard M.	"	Reyburn, Thomas G.	"
Hardesty, Henry	"	Riggs, George	"
Hauce, James	"	Steever, Daniel	"
Hamilton, James, jr.	"	Smith, George	"
Hart, Henry	"	Sultzer, Sebastian	"
Hart, William	"	Smith, John S.	"
Jenkins, Wm. C.	"	Shortridge, John	"
Jenkins, James	"	Swetzer, Samuel	"
Kurtz, Charles	"	Swetzer, Seth	"
Keener, John	"	Thompson, Wm.	"
Lee, James H.	"	Talbot, Edward	"
Leigh, Wm.	"	Thompson, James	"
Levely, Wm.	"	Thompson, Thomas	"
Lawson, Richard	"	Tustin, Samuel	"
Long, Reuben	"	Torrence, John	"
Larsh, Charles	"	Trimble, Joshua	"
Lucas, Harrison	"	Uhler, George	"
Maulsby, Israel D.	"	Vance, John	"
Middleton, Richard	"	Wilson, Edward M.	"
Myers, Thomas	"	Wilson, John	"
Montieth, John	"	Wilson, Thomas	"
Morreson, P. V.	"	White, John	"
Murry, Matthew	"	Whelan, Thomas	"
Martin, James	"	Welsh, William	"
Miller, Benj. H.	"	Ward, John W.	"
Miltenberger, Anthony	"	Woods, Wm. H.	"
Moore, Robt. S.	"	Woods, Andrew H.	"
Nouvell, Michael	"	Werger, Michael	"
Norris, Luther A.	"	Williams, Thomas	"
Norris, Samuel	"	Tilyard, William	"
Nagle, Anthony	"	Wills, Francis	"
Norris, Benjamin	"		

Names of the Field and Staff and Company Officers, Non-Commissioned Officers and Privates of the Sixth Regiment of the Maryland Militia who served at North Point and Fort McHenry 12th September, 1814—taken from the Muster Rolls on file in the office of the Third Auditor of the Treasury of the United States:

WILLIAM MCDONALD, *Lieutenant Colonel.*
THOMAS TENANT, 1st *Major.*
WILLIAM PECHIN, 2d *Major.*
JAMES BIAYS, JR., *Adjutant.*
JOHN SNYDER, *Pay Master.*
ALEXANDER CUMMINS, *Quarter Master.*
JOSEPH ALLENDER, *Surgeon.*
HENRY JOHNSON, *Surgeon's Mate.*
WILLIAM HOULTON, *Sergeant Major.*
WALTER SIMPSON, *Quarter Master Sergeant.*

Thomas Sheppard, Captain.	Craggs, Robert	Private.
William Evans, 1st Lieutenant.	Cooper, John	"
Peter Chailie, Ensign.	Chailie, Stephen	"
James I. Rigby, Sergeant.	Costolo, Andrew	"
James I. Costole, do.	Dunham, Jacob	"
Cornelius B. Long, do.	Denny, William	"
Daniel Evans, do.	Day, Lerey	"
Samuel Wilson, Corporal.	Davidson, William	"
Daniel Perigo, do.	Etchberger, William	"
Patrick Cooney, do.	Evans, Westley	"
John Peal, Principal Musician.	Fenby, Samuel	"
Ja'b Zorne, do.	Fenby, Peter, jr.	"
Arnold, William Private.	Frazure, Jeremiah	"
Atwell, Nathaniel "	Feilds, James	"
Allen, Adam T. "	Graff, John	"
Armitage, Jonas "	Graff, Jacob	"
Biays, Joseph "	Grieves, James	"
Bready, Jason "	Green, Peter	"
Baldwin, Abram "	Gray, Walter	"
Bratcher, William "	Hunter, Isaac	"
Bandell, William "	Hunt, Benjamin	"
Boss, John "	Houlton, John	"
Bready, Israel "	James, Levi	"
Bandell, John "	Kolehouse, Lawr'ce G.	"
Bell, James "	Klock, John	"
Baker, James "	Krebbs, George	"
Baker, Benjamin "	Ling, Robert	"
Bandell, George "	Lauderman, Fred'k	"
Brown, Garrett "	Little, James	"
Bateman, Amzi "	McMackon, Alex'r	"

McCafferty, John	Private.	Shaw, Samuel H.	Private.
Peters, Christian G.	"	Smith, J. Job	"
Pilkington, Thomas	"	Smith, James P.	"
Philips, Nathaniel	"	Stewart, James	"
Plummer, Benj'n C.	"	Shaffer, James	"
Quisic, John	"	Smith, John	"
Reed, Robert	"	Tridle, Jacob	"
Ross, David	"	White, James	"
Rogers, David	"	Warnkin, Henry	"
Ruster, Lewis	"	Wagoner, George	"
Rockhold, Charles	"	Weary, John	"
Stretch, Samuel	"	Willis, Joshua	"

Gerrard Wilson, Captain.		Holmes, Thomas	Private.
William Inloes, 1st Lieut.		Holmes, Vincent	"
Isaac Atkinson, Ensign.		Horseman, Charles	"
T. W. Brotherton, 1st Ser'gt.		Hammet, Jesse	"
John Pickett,	2d do.	Hooker, James	"
Lewis C. Muller,	3d do.	Jones, Jas. D.	"
John Fosset,	4th do.	Jackson, Major	"
Henry Delaha,	1st Corp'l.	Joynes, Leonard	"
Morris Morris,	2d do.	Jones, William	"
Samuel Coleman,	3d do.	Litten, Thomas	"
Owen Morris,	4th do.	League, Abraham	"
Ralph Wane, Drummer.		Lawrence, Joseph	"
Abbot, William	Private.	Leahy, John	"
Abbot, Michael	"	Larkin, William	"
Adams, Nathl.	"	Madary, William	"
Armstrong, Solomon	"	McElroy, John	"
Brown, John	"	Mettee, Martin	"
Buck, Samuel	"	McMullen, Nathl.	"
Brunket, William	"	Metz, George	"
Brown, Hugh	"	McLaughlin, Jo.	"
Caughry, Bernard	"	Moss, Barney	"
Camerly, John	"	McCollister, Richard	"
Cascaden, Robert	"	Mitchell, William	"
Camerly, Peter	"	Nelson, Basil	"
Coleman, Richard	"	Newbury, John	"
Crawford, John	"	Palmer, Isaac	"
Cole, J. A.	"	Pitch, Samuel !	"
Cork, John	"	Ritter, Jacob	"
Dowling, William	"	Roberts, Owen	"
Dougherty, Barney	"	Robinson, Joseph	"
Danerson, Richard	"	Sexton, Charles	"
Donelly, Daniel	"	Steffer, Frederick	"
Foster, Jacob	"	Shane, Michael	"
Forester, George	"	Taylor, Thomas	"
Galloway, John	"	Taylor, James	"
Gorsic, Thomas	"	Thomas, Abel	"

Wright, Richd.	Private.	Wellslager, Jacob	Private.
Weater, George	"	Walker, Jacob	"
Wren, James	"	Williamson, Jas.	"

Peter Galt, Captain.		Johnston, Mathias	Private.
Nichs. Brewer, Lieutenant.		King, James	"
Richd. Pindall, Ensign.		Keatley, Richard	"
Richd. Bell, 1st Serg't.		Kneppenburg, Andw.	"
Richd. Parrot, 2d do.		Lastie, John	"
John Echburger, 3d do.		Leaf, Johnzee	"
Wm. Williamson, 4th do.		Lenox, William	"
Charles Fox, 1st Corp'l.		Lobby, Lewis	"
Jas H. Thomas, 2d do.		Long, John	"
James Smith, 3d do.		Landragan, Phillup	"
John Stickney, 4th do.		Mahue, William	"
Atwell, John	Private.	Porter, Thos.	"
Albertis, Willm.	"	Potter, David	"
Bradbury, Stephen	"	Parsons, John D.	"
Beard, Henry	"	Powell, William	"
Crozier, Willm.	"	Reeves, John	"
Crea, Hugh	"	Rolph, Neal	"
Crea, James	"	Ringrose, James	"
Curteau, Wm.	"	Sherwood, Phillup	"
Cherbert, Chs. F.	"	Sunderland, Wm.	"
Carpenter, Geo.	"	Smith, Edwd.	"
Deal, William	"	Smith, Adam	"
Drummond, Jas.	"	Sleekum, Peter	"
Evans, Daniel	"	Street, Richard	"
Foster, Joseph	"	Strickland, Henry	"
Foulds, William	"	Stephens, John	"
Fernandis, Anthony	"	Turner, Isaac	"
Gardner, Kensey	"	Townsend, Dennad	"
Grace, John	"	Waltham, Wm.	"
Gochear, Anthony	"	Winstanley, John	"
Hatch, Samuel	"	Weatherby, Thos.	"
Hudson, John	"	Weatherby, Elisha	"
Hinton, Dennis	"	Wirt, Jacob	"
Harrison, William	"	Wampler, Nathl.	"
Johns, Isaac D.	"	Wolf, Henry	"
Johns, Richard	"	White, Joseph	"

William Brown, Captain.	John Slater, Serg't.
R. D. Millholand, Lieutenant.	Robert Cooper, do.
James Weaver, Ensign.	Corsey H. Edward, do.
Thos. Gallaway, 1st Serg't.	Jesse Boston, Corp'l.
Alex. Cummins, Q. M. S.	Clay Arquith, do.

Joseph Gollibert, Corp'l.
Samuel Watts, do.
Atkinson, John Private.
Allen, John "
Bennett, Matthew "
Bonfield, Thomas "
Bowen, Martin "
Baker, Giddie "
Bunbury, Henry "
Bryan, Joseph "
Claridge, Levin "
Cadel, John "
Cassen, John "
Carroll, Robert "
Clary, Michael "
Cochran, Michael "
Caswell, John "
Donnelly, Simon "
Dayley, John "
Degilver, John "
Davis, Abraham "
Denson, James "
Fish, James "
Grimes, Levi "
Griffin, Henry "
Graham, Wm. "
Griffen, Benjn. "
Goodwin, John "
Harrison, Henry "
Hatcherson, Thos. "
Hurst, George "
Harper, Peter "
Humphries, John "
Justis, Morton, "

Kierl, John W. Private.
Kermichael, Wm. "
Kerby, Thomas "
Lauderman, Geo. "
Long, Jacob "
Lemmon, Henry "
McCoy, John "
Muer, Thomas "
Morris, John "
Miller, James "
Pamphilion, Edward "
Quin, Edward "
Strustrum, Magnus "
Sweer, Peter "
Slater, Alexr, "
Stradler, John "
Stevens, Darius "
Swager, William "
Travers, William "
Turner, Caleb "
Tuel, Martin "
Thornton, Sergeod "
Tumbleson, Wm. "
Tunnell, Isaiah "
Williams, Isaac "
Webb, John "
Wright, Walter "
Wiley, William "
Wolf, Frederick "
Wright, Edward "
Weary, William "
Wigley, William "
Winwright, John "

Thos. L. Lawrence, Captain.
John Burk, Lieutenant.
Joshua Atkinson, Ensign.
John G. Chappell, do.
Samuel Harrison, Serg't.
William Cathrill, do.
Patrick Gallaspy, do.
Thomas Price, do.
C. C. Bobart, Corp'l.
Thomas Smith, do.
Benjamin Boyle, do.
Samuel Hawney, do.
James League, Drummer.

Abry, Christopher Private.
Anderson, William "
Belton, John "
Boston, Isaac "
Boyd, Matthew "
Briscoe, James "
Barlow, John "
Burke, David, jr. "
Carey, Joseph "
Carr, Nicholas "
Cammeron, John "
Cannada, Ebenezer "
Cole, Frederick "

Coleman, Joseph	Private.	Martin, Joseph	Private.
Cunningham, Joseph	"	Martin, John	"
Clyne, Daniel D.	"	Mickle, John	"
Davis, Thomas	"	Moon, Allen	"
Davis, Joshua	"	Mayher, Timothy D.	"
Donaldson, Jesse	"	Philips, George	"
Doyle, Patrick	"	Rigo, Clement	"
Dempsey, John	"	Robinson, Thomas	"
Evans, Thomas	"	Robinson, John	"
Eachburger, Jacob	"	Radish, Thomas	"
Easton, Nicholas	"	Rains, Lewis	"
Furguson, William	"	Rice, Edward	"
Freeman, John	"	Smith, John E.	"
Gardner, George	"	Sky, Gattiel	"
Gale, William	"	Sollers, John	"
Griffith, David	"	Stebeck, John	"
Gray, John	"	Scott, Robert	"
Gunby, Stephen	"	Stansbury, Nicholas	"
Harwood, Benjamin	"	Strand, John	"
Hooper, James	"	Sinclair, Perry	"
Hamilton, John	"	Sterrett, Alexander	"
Hammond, Joseph	"	Saiman, Joseph	"
Harrison, Thomas	"	Thomas, Thomas	"
Inloes, John	"	Thompson, James	"
Johnson, Charles	"	Traverse, Henry	"
Kivens, Samuel	"	Tincler, W. P.	"
King, Thomas, jr.	"	Tucker, William	"
Lock, Washington	"	Thompson, William	"
Leoni, G. C.	"	Williams, Giles	"

Benjamin Ringold, Captain.
Robert D. Allen, Lieutenant.
Joseph Hart, Ensign.
John B Hall, Serg't.
John Mansfield, do.
John Thomas, do.
Peter Zane, do.
Samuel Burnes, Corp'l.
Edwin H. Alford, do.
Jacob Winchester, do.
Amos Chapman, do.
Allender, John   Private.
Alexander, Joseph   "
Billington, James   "
Booth, William   "
Bankson, James   "
Batchelor, Nathaniel   "
Byrne, Lawrence   "

Comegys, Jesse   Private.
Comegys, Cornelius   "
Carroll, Aquilla   "
Cross, Andrew   "
Carr, John   "
Calvin, Richard   "
Clayton, Samuel   "
Chrisfield, Samuel   "
Canney, John   "
Dopt, George   "
Dutton, John   "
Davit, William   "
Dawson, William   "
Dinsmore, John   "
Ellis, Thomas   "
Eccle, John   "
Eades, Thomas   "
Fales, Benjamin   "

Gill, Selmon	Private.	Matthews, William	Private.
Gooding, Jones	"	Merryman, Samuel	"
Gooding, Marmaduke	"	McConkey, William	"
Graham, William	"	Obrien, Francis	"
Hudson, James	"	Patterson, William	"
Hindes, John	"	Plummer, James	"
Hutton, Joseph	"	Robinson, David	"
Hamilton, John	"	Reddon, George	"
Hewit, Elmer	"	Rigdon, William	"
Herbert, Thomas	"	Rutter, William	"
Hussey, Joseph	"	Stallings, Aquilla	"
Hatton, Hagerty	"	Schroder, John	"
Hughes, Vincent	"	Slater, Benjamin	"
Howlet, John	"	Steel, Penson	"
Kitchcart, John	"	Salques, Selah	"
Kellum, James	"	Tucker, Joseph	"
Lewis, Lewis D.	"	Taylor, William	"
Lovedet, John	"	Towsley, William	"
McClellen, Matthew	"	Uhler, Frederick	"
McClain, John	"	Vanhorn, Fielding	"
Mann, George	"	Valentine, Arch. K.	"
Muratte, Samuel	"	Williams, James	"
Merrit, Samuel	"	Walker, John	"
Maxwell, Joshua	"	Williams, William	"
Mann, James	"	Washington, Lawrence	"
Mitchell, John	"	Yager, John	"
Mitchell, Richard	"		

Luke Kienstead, Captain.		Dunn, James	Private.
Wm. Hubbard, Lieutenant.		Denning, Spry	"
Davis McCaughan, Ensign.		Fingan, James	"
Jos. Robinson, 1st Serg't.		Glass, John	"
Thos. Willender, 2d do.		Gray, Andrew	"
Conrad Switzer, 3d do.		Gerrand, Ibram	"
Barney Lerich, 4th do.		Glasby, John	"
Moses Desent, 1st Corp'l.		Hall, Lewis	"
Curtis Dunn, 2d do.		Harden, Thomas	"
Perigrine Ward, 3d do.		Hubert, Thomas	"
John Parsons, 4th do.		Hunt, John	"
Boza, John	Private.	Jones, Barren	"
Burgis, John	"	Kemp, Joseph	"
Benson, Stephen	"	Kholehouse, Fred'k	"
Cock, Solomon	"	Kemp, Thomas	"
Cline, David	"	Kerby, Samuel	"
Caprice, Joseph	"	Kell, Flemming	"
Cowles, William	"	Leach, Henry	"
Cole, Thomas	"	Mason, James	"
Desent, George	"	McCleanley, John	"
Dorman, William	"	McBean, Angus	"

Morris, James	Private.	Sute, John		Private.
Mason, Abraham,	"	Todd, Samuel		"
Pierce, Joseph	"	Tims, Benjamin		"
Peacock, William	"	Wilson, James		"
Peel, George	"	Williams, John		"
North, Edward	"	Woods, John		"
Sablis, Michael	"	Willing, Henry		"
Smith, William	"	Zane, Joseph		"

Sam'l McDonald, Captain.		Dennis, John	Private.
James Biays, jr., Lieutenant.		Eagleston, John	"
Hugh Allen, Ensign.		Fenton, John	"
Robert Dempsey,	1st Serg't.	Goodwin, Caleb	"
Joseph Graham,	2d do.	Gray, John	"
Thos. Brankan,	3d do.	Hague, Joseph	"
Jona. Townsend,	4th do.	Harrison, Joseph	"
James Sinclair,	1st Corp'l.	Heary, David	"
William Askew,	2d do.	Harrison, Thomas	"
Henry Middleton,	3d do.	Harrison, Samuel	"
Wm. Wilkenson,	4th do.	Harrison, Nicholas	"
Adams, Robert	Private.	Kelby, Samuel	"
Atwell, William	"	Kensy, Peter	"
Arnold, John	"	Lanman, Daniel	"
Alexander, William	"	Leach, John	"
Bowline, Roger	"	Macey, William	"
Berton, Nicholas	"	McLane, Charles	"
Blades, George	"	Matthews, John	"
Baine, John	"	Miles, Benjamin	"
Broom, Thomas	"	McGraw, Thomas	"
Burke, John	"	Neven, Thomas	"
Calif, John	"	Pantry, John	"
Calif, James	"	Papyon, John	"
Cummings, Robert	"	Read, John	"
Christopher, Charles	"	Sinclair, Alexander	"
Carroll, John	"	Stewman, William	"
Davy, Henry	"	Teal, Archibald	"
Denny, John	"	Williams, George	"
Disney, William	"	Wilson, George	"

Robert Conway, Captain.		George Lee, Corporal.	
Robert Graves, Lieutenant.		James Slater, do.	
Thomas Cornthwait, Ensign.		John Ellis, do.	
Lewis Auodoun, Serg't.		Lewis Ellis, do.	
Thomas Burke, do.		Adam, William	Private.
Joseph Tharp, do.		Airs, Samuel	"
Edward Clemens, do.		Baxter, Colin	"

Blades, John	Private.	Reese, George	Private.
Broom, Henry	"	Remman, Philip	"
Broom, John	"	Rogers, Patrick	"
Butler, John	"	Ramsey, John	"
Clarck, John	"	Rider, Joshua	"
Clarck, George	"	Ramsey, Thomas	"
Cooper, Elisha	"	Redgraves, Samuel	"
Caperlinde, Nicholas	"	Ready, Samuel	"
Fisher, Caleb	"	Stites, William	"
Flanagan, Hugh	"	Snyder, Joseph	"
Heard, John	"	Smith, William	"
Jones, John	"	Southcomb, Peter	"
Jennings, Daniel	"	Sanders, George	"
Lloyd, John	"	Wigley, Henry	"
Lynch, Abraham	"	Walstern, Samuel	"
Luberg, John	"	Waddam, George	"
Mace, Thomas	"	Williams, John	"
McCubbin, William	"	Yam, Thomas	"
McGurch, John	"	Zigler, George	"

Nicholas Burke, Captain.		Fishwick, John	Private.
Thomas Reardon, Lieutenant.		Fisher, James	"
Michael Bandel, Ensign.		Farland, John	"
Samuel Boyde,	1st Serg't.	Gamble, John	"
Joseph Hill,	2d do.	Gilman, John	"
Frederick Cole,	3d do.	Hopkins, Greenbury	"
Thos. Harrington,	4th do.	Holton, David	"
John Wane,	1st Corp'l.	Haerfnagle, John	"
John Murphy,	2d do.	Hanson, Nicholas	"
W. M. Connokin,	3d do.	Hinton, Robert W	"
Jacob Burke,	4th do.	Jones, Even	"
Anderson, John	Private.	Lewis, James	"
Bradshaw, Thomas	"	Leatherbury, Thomas	"
Bandel, Frederick	"	McWilliams, Hugh	"
Carter, John S	"	Mahaney, John	"
Creemer, Joshua	"	Marshall, Matthias	"
Cole, William	"	Morgan, John W	"
Claradge, Henry	"	Ogden, Nathaniel J.	"
Callender, James	"	Owens, James	"
Campble, James	"	Rockhold, Asel	"
Collins, John	"	Riggen, Benton	"
Cook, Leaven	"	Sprague, Henry	"
Dempsey, John	"	Speak, Nicholas	"
Duvall, Washington	"	Saldge, Conrod	"
Elliott, John P	"	Thomas, William	"
Elliott, John	"	Taylor, John	"
Ellender, Frederick	"	Turfield, Philip	"
Elliott, Thomas W	"	Vanhorn, James	"

Varnor, Robert	Private.	Wheeler, Austin	Private.
Wells, Isaac	"	West, Amos	"
Waites, James D.	"	Wilkins, William	"
Waites, Richard	"		

John G. Dixon, Captain.
Brooklin Terry, 1st Lieut.
Henry Heckratte, 2d do.
John Sutton, Ensign.
Wm. Heckratte, 1st Serg't.
Chaun'y Hurlbut, 2d do.
David Brown, 3d do.
Thomas Faulkner, 4th do.
John Plumb, Drummer.
Letus Sackett, Fifer.
Anderson, Jordan Private.
Ackworth, Train "
Buzzard, Peter "
Blunt, Erastus "
Crya, Adam "
Carlile, Samuel "
Caddock, Elisha "
Drum, Henry "
Bayd, Dinsman "

Drum, David Private.
Dougherty, John "
Dick, John C "
Dorcas, John "
Evans, John "
Gaskill, Cripps "
Hillman, Aaron "
Henderson, James "
Langstorpp, Daniel "
Lightner, Joseph "
McClure, Randel "
McMullin, John "
McMullin, James "
Marsh, Henry "
Marlin, David "
Robinson, George "
Stine, Isaac "
Scarpass, Frederick "
Wain, George "

Names of the Field and Staff and Company Officers, Non-Commissioned Officers and Privates of the twenty-seventh Regiment of Maryland Militia, who served at North Point and Fort McHenry, 12th September, 1814—taken from the Muster Rolls, on file in the Office of the Third Auditor of the Treasury of the United States.

KENNEDY LONG, *Lieutenant Colonel.*
SAMUEL MOORE, 1*st Major.*
JOSEPH ROBINSON, 2*d Major.*
JAMES L. DONALDSON, *Lieutenant and Adjutant.*
HENRY M. FISHER, *Lieutenant and Quarter Master.*
JAMES L. DAWES, *Lieutenant and Pay Master.*
THOMAS HAMILTON, *Surgeon.*
EDWARD H. WORRELL, *Surgeon's Mate.*
GEORGE CRAIG, *Sergeant Major.*
JOHN L. COOK, *Quarter Master's Sergeant.*

James McConkey, Captain.
Abraham Scott, Lieutenant.
Ebenezer Swain, Ensign.
Geo. Miltenberger, Serg't.
Charles Barker, do.
John Warren, do.
John Hicks, do.
Jacob H. Lawton, Corp'l.
John Lackey, do.
Franklin Edmonson, do.
Nicholas Ridgely, do.
Allen, John Private.
Ash, Lewis "
Ashmead, Hosea "
Askew, Robert "
Austin, John "
Allen, Thomas "
Butler, William "
Biddle, Abraham "
Blunt, Samuel "
Boyce, Charles "
Burns, James "
Berger, John "
Barrett, Thomas "
Carty, John "
Chapman, Joseph "
Cain, Claiburn "
Connard, Frederick "
Chrisfield, Perry "
Collins, William "
Dorr, Leonard "
Dykes, Joseph "
Davies, Samuel "
Estel, James B. "
Fannon, William "
Fowler, John "
Foster, James "
Gossen, Henry "
Goddard, Charles "
Gray, Zacharia R. "
Gordon, Joseph "
Griffin, Luther "
Hagen, Michael "
Heron, Alexander "
Hare, Jesse "
Heslip, John "
Hill, Alexander "
Hinkley, William "
Jeffrey, Richard "
Jeffrey, Robert "
Johnson, Deter "

Jennings, Samuel Private.
Jones, William "
Kurtzs, John "
Keetch, Robert "
Kurtzs, Robert "
Kerr, William "
Lanham, John "
Labborrie, Nicholas "
Lee, George "
Lawton, John "
McChristal, John "
McFarland, John "
McPherson, Thomas "
McCann, Thomas "
McGoldrick, John "
McChristal, James "
McChristal, Patrick "
Maguire, John "
Mace, Thomas "
Mattocks, George "
Miskelly, Peter "
Moss, Charles "
Neale, James G. W. "
Oliver, Amos "
Orum, Edward "
O'Donnell, Barney "
Parker, Richard B. "
Paul, Thomas "
Pouge, Loudy I. "
Prichard, Cyrus "
Palmetary, John H. "
Pugh, David "
Roberts, Edward B. "
Richards, David "
Ray, Francis "
Ross, James "
Rust, Samuel "
Rogers, William "
Rhyhnhart, Ezekiel "
Rigby, Edward "
Sinclair, Matthew "
Saulsby, John "
Smith, William "
Smith, Thomas "
Spencer, Reuben "
Sprigg, Edward "
Spurrier, John "
Stephens, Alexander "
Supper, John "
Stiger, Peter "
Summers, George "

Skelton, John	Private.	Woolen, William	Private.
Steevers, Adam	"	Wolf, Isaac	"
Taylor, Levi	"	Waterman, Warren	"
Taylor, George	"	Wray, John	"
West, Richard	"	Welsh, Daniel	"
Wilson, Thomas	"	Stephen Brown, Capt. Servt.	
Wilson, Thomas L	"		

John Kennedy, Captain.
William Lafferty, Lieutenant.
William Buck, Ensign.
Jacob Craft,   1st Serg't.
Conrod Keller, 2d   do.
Hillery Elder, 3d   do.
Hy. Freeburger, 4th   do.
Henry Huber, 2d Corp'l.
Henry Rust,   4th do.

Alford, Thomas,	Private.	Gillum, Simon	Private.
Beard, Alexander	"	Griffith, John	"
Busey, Charles	"	Griswold, Livy	"
Bailer, Hezekiah	"	Haslett, Charles	"
Benner, James	"	Hunt, Jesse	"
Bende, George	"	Hopkins, Richard	"
Bruner, Elias	"	Jacobs, Benjamin	"
Brisco, Benjamin	"	Kennon, John B	"
Brocas, John	"	Knox, James	"
Batty, Philip	"	Knox, John	"
Calvert, William	"	Little, John	"
Conner, Edward	"	Lewellin, John	"
Callihan, Peter	"	More, John	"
Clark, John	"	Mapp, William	"
Cole, Andrew	".	McDonald, James	"
Childs, Thomas	"	McDaniel, Daniel	"
Cole, John	"	McKinzie, Thomas	"
Chapman, George	"	Miles, Joshua	"
Deshields, William	"	Murry, Thomas	"
Daniel, James	"	McGruder, Samuel	"
Delano, Judah	"	Pain, Richard	"
During, James	"	Paschal, Jeremiah	"
Dougherty, James	"	Palmetery, John	"
Dun, James	"	Quest, Charles	"
Duffy, Hugh	"	Ritchardson, James	"
Davidson, Nelson	"	Rapley, Abraham	"
Etsberger, William	"	Russel, Samuel	"
Elder, Samuel	"	Ray, Andrew	"
Fordice, John	"	Riley, John	"
Fairbank, William	"	Specht, Cornelius	"
Ferrel, Francis	"	Smewings, James	"
		Stansbury, William	"
		Spencer, William	"
		Sheamer, James	"
		Storks, Levy	"
		Taylor, John	"
		Taylor, Thomas A.	"
		Warner, Alfred L	"
		Wilson, Thomas	"
		Welch, John G	"

James Dillon, Captain.
Jas. F. Winchell, 1st Lieut.
John Lester, Ensign.
Isaac N. Toy, 1st Serg't.
John Williams, 2d do.
Benj. F. Pollock, 3d do.
William Kelly, 4th do.
Caleb Pasterfield, Corp'l.
George Catts, do.
Nathaniel Creaver, do.
Joseph Purden, do.
Ryan, William Private.
Martin, Joseph "
Teppish, Caspar "
Alexander, John "
Brown, James "
Brady, Michael "
Buckley, James "
Barton, Isaac "
Barnes, Bennet H. "
Burnes, Charles "
Bentzle, Frederick "
Carnes, William "
Curry, Isaac "
Carter, Jesse "
Carroll, N. C. "
Cappuch, William "
Chaney, Cornelius "
Cross, John "
Carroll, William "
Cochran, George "
Deems, John "
Daley, John "
Dorsey, Vachel "
Ditten, David "
Doddrell, J. C. "
Eisenhart, J. D. "
Eddy, Rufus "
Eden, William "
Fisher, William "
Gray, James "

Glenn. Samuel Private.
Gibson, Samuel "
Gomley, Richard "
Gorsuch, Joshua "
Harryman, S. "
Hamilton, Robert "
Hicks, Elijah "
Hinton, Thomas "
Harr, William "
Jephson, John "
Jones, Robinson "
Jacobs, James "
Kneeland, Richard "
Kelsner, John "
Koch, Henry "
McNeilly, Jeremiah "
McJilton, William "
Murray, William "
Myers, Henry "
Mintz, Seth "
Nugent, Neal "
Neal, John "
Pacack, John "
Plintenberger, Chas. "
Potter, Martin "
Pencast, Asa "
Philips, Edward "
Powell, P. B. "
Rumbaugh, Peter "
Roston, William "
Richardson, Jabes "
Rust, Abraham "
Smith, George "
Tucker, James "
Thompson, David "
Turpin, Sacka "
Wade, George "
Wadlow, John "
Walton, Nathaniel "
Wan, James "
Wilson, Peter "

Benjamin Edes, Captain,
Samuel G. Hyde, Lieutenant.
Joseph Jackson, Ensign.
Walter Theker, 1st Serg't.
Rich'd Bradshaw, 2d do.
Robert Bell, 3d do.
William Reeves, 4th do.

Rd. Diffenderffer, 1st Corp'l.
Thomas Dryden, 2d do.
Frederick Cole, 3d do.
Edward Beackly, 4th do.
Aborn, John Private.
Allen, John "
Butler, Absalom "

Barney, Wheaton J.	Private.	Lemonth, Alexander	Private.
Blanch, Thomas	"	Lewis, Shraddrack	"
Buchanan, Francis	"	Labroche, Barnabas	"
Bintzell, Baltzer	"	Longford, John	"
Bringman, Thomas	"	Leard, Samuel	"
Burke, Joshua	"	Marvin, Clarr	"
Conner, Abraham	"	McConkey, William	"
Connell, Bartholomew	"	Mackey, James	"
Collins, Thomas	"	McCoy, James	"
Casserd, Lewis	"	McCain, Charles	"
Cadle, Daniel	"	Morris, Jesse	"
Chase, Philip W.	"	Madison, Thomas	"
Dryden, Littleton D.	"	McGee, John	"
Devos, John	"	Mackey, William	"
Daugherty, Samuel	"	Montgomery, John	"
Estis, Thomas	"	Prill, Henry	"
Earley, John	"	Pearson, Thomas	"
Evans, Joseph	"	Phelps, Greenbury	"
Estell, John	"	Prosser, Samuel	"
Fish, Allen	"	Prosser, Uriah	"
Fendall, Edward	"	Roy, John	"
Grewe, Henry W.	"	Richards, John	"
Guest, Thomas	"	Rodman, Robert R.	"
Green, Edward	"	Stendham, Peter A.	"
Giddings, Benj.	"	Stevens, John	"
Gladding, Samuel	"	Sullivan, John	"
Gorsuch, Nicholas	"	Smith, Thomas	"
Griffith, Henry B.	"	Stevens, Mark	"
Henderson, John	"	Stocker, Charles	"
Hopewell, Hugh	"	Sinton, Joseph	"
Hull, William	"	Taylor, Henry	"
Hays, Robert	"	Thomas, John	"
Hutchinson, William	"	Urie, Jeremiah	"
Hadaway, Robert	"	Vanbaun, William	"
Johnston, Joseph	"	Wise, Augustus	"
Jordan, Robert	"	Wilson, John	"
Jervis, William	"	Wooles, Stephen	"
Ireland, John F.	"	Wallace, Thomas	"
Kennedy, James	"	Williams, James	"
Key, Abner	"	Yerkess, Anthony	"
Keichcoff, George	"		

John McKane, Captain.		John Pyfer,	1st Corp'l.
Daniel Crook, Lieutenant.		Bernard Dupuy,	2d do.
Francis Morton, Ensign.		Christo'r. Wynn,	3d do.
Thomas G Hill,	1st Serg't.	William Jackson,	4th do
Curtis Sheldon,	2d do.	Armstrong, Robert	Private.
John Muderwood,	3d do.	Avery, Jonathan	"
Richard Lenox,	4th do.	Belt, Joseph	"

Bollman, Thomas	Private.	Lewis, John	Private.
Beale, Nathan	"	Long, Levi	"
Bowers, John	"	Lloyd, William	"
Burneston, Joseph, jr.	"	McCoy, William	"
Briar, Emanuel	"	McClane, Elias	"
Bonner, John	"	Moffit, Noah	"
Burden, Samuel	"	McNeir, John	"
Clarke, William	"	Markland, James	"
Crawley, Samuel	"	Monsarrat, Nicholas	"
Craig, James	"	McIlvain, George	"
Crumwell, Michael	"	McKinley, William	"
Collins, William	"	Mattocks, William	"
Conway, Robert	"	Mickle, Robert	"
Connelly, Bernard	"	McHenry, F. D.	"
Duffy, Henry	"	Neale, Benjamin	"
Donnell, John	"	O'Donnell, Patrick	"
Dougherty, John	"	Oldham, Elisha	"
Elbert, Samuel	"	O'Brien, James	"
Goldsmith, John	"	Perry, Jeremiah	"
Gwynn, William	"	Pattridge, James	"
Gray, Nicholas	"	Poulnat, John	"
Gale, Lewis	"	Peters, James	"
Gardner, Peter	"	Reed, John	"
Hebb, Henry	"	Reinagle, Thomas	"
Hayward, John	"	Reintzel, George	"
Hall, John	"	Riggin, Levi	"
Harris, S. W.	"	Ratliff, Gilbert	"
Hawley, Irza	"	Reed, Patrick	"
Hall, Henry	"	Riley, John S.	"
Herbert, William P	"	Stockman, Jacob	"
Hall, George	"	Stewart, John N.	"
Hoyt, Reuben	"	Smith, Robert	"
Johns, James	"	Smith, Cyrus	"
James, George	"	Smith, David	"
Jones, Daniel	"	Sloan, James, jr.	"
Kaminskie, John C.	"	Toelle, Garrard	"
Kelly, Thomas	"	Taylor, William	"
Levy, Vincent	"	Tanner, Samuel	"
Lampley, John M	"	Underwood, John, jr.	"
Lee, Thomas	"	Wills, Richard	"
Littig, Philip	"	Wilson, Hosea	"
Lucas, Fielding, jr.	"	Watson, Robert	"

Peter Pinney, Captain,   William Powell, 4th do.
Samuel Legrand, Lieutenant.   Robt. B. Varden, 1st Corp'l.
Joseph Towson, Ensign.   Thomas Fox, 2d do.
Alling Sergeant, 1st Serg't.   James Dalrymple, 3d do.
Samuel Hadley, 2d do.   Jacob Cable, 4th do.
Elisha Lewis, 3d do.   George Teal, Musician.

Arnold, Francis	Private.	Joy, Edward	Private.
Arnold, Peter	"	Johnson, John	"
Ball, James	"	Johnson, James	"
Brewer, John R	"	Keirl, Matthew	"
Bond, William	"	Knorr, William	"
Brown, Paoli	"	Livingston, James	"
Bond, Charles	"	Marshall, Andrew	"
Boon, Benjamin	"	Morgan, Jesse	"
Batteau, Christian	"	McKenzie, James	"
Brown, John	"	Medcalf, William	"
Beecham, Thomas	"	Mopps, Frederick	"
Beatty, Samuel	"	Mearis, Jacob	"
Carroll, James	"	Newon, Patrick	"
Cheston, William	"	Niles, Hezekiah	"
Cale, Daniel	"	Nippard, George	"
Cook, John L.	"	Ogden, David	"
Duddy, Henry	"	Patridge, Job	"
Davis, Charles	"	Parrish, Isaac	"
Desk, Michael	"	Powell, James	"
Dewling, Wiliam	"	Pearce, William	"
Dixon, William	"	Rouse, George	"
Evans, John	"	Rogers, George	"
Falknier, Abraham	"	Reese, John	"
Finney, Lewis	"	Robinson, John M.	"
Gamble, Darius	"	Rial, Absalom	"
Glenn, Elijah	"	Riley, Valerius	"
Gray, William	"	Shyrach, Charles	"
Hugg, Richard	"	Spencer, Robert	"
Howard, William	"	Thompson, John	"
Hayley, Henry	"	Toulson, Thomas	"
Hibbert, Solomon	"	Tittle, Jeremiah	"
Hoffman, George W.	"	Trickett, John	"
Hauptman, John	"	Wallace, James	"
Hamilton, James	"		

George Steever, Captain.		Baty, Oliver	Private.
James May, Lieutenant.		Browning, William	"
Jeremiah Green, Ensign.		Baker, David	"
Joseph Sewell, Serg't.		Cox, Jonathan	"
John Conner, do.		Carter, Charles	"
Phillip Gatch, do.		Cook, John W.	"
Isaac Burke, do.		Carter, John	"
John Wisham, Corp'l.		Dungan, William	"
Alexander Sinley, do.		Dillahunt, Thomas	"
Frederick Baker, do.		Deverix, John	"
Amos, John	Private.	Delsher, William	"
Baifield, James	"	Daugherty, Charles	"
Birmingham, John	"	Edes, John	"
Burk, Richard	"	Eli, George	

Fornsbill, John	Private.	Reading, John	Private.
Graves, John	"	Rothrock, Jacob	"
Gorsuch, Thomas	"	Romney, Robert	"
Hiss, Philip	"	Roan, George H.	"
Hatten, Aquilla	"	Rust, William	"
Hatten, Calup	"	Stansbury, Aug. M.	"
Jones, Malon	"	Stansbury, David	"
Jones, Hugh S.	"	Smith, George	"
Jeffries, William	"	Sliver, John	"
Jennings, John	"	Stemmin, Barnard	'
Kent, Robert	"	Saunders, Bend't. J.	"
Love, Joseph	"	Thompson, James	"
League, Nathan	"	Taylor, Archibald	"
Long, Henry	"	Vansant, Christopher	"
Logan, John B.	"	Vanberger, John	"
Little, William	"	Wisbaugh, Martin	"
Lawless, John	"	Wheeler, Thomas	"
Leforge, Clarkson	"	Witterfield, James	"
Lightner, George	"	White, Allen	"
Magauran, Henry	"	Woilds, David	"
McCoy, Samuel	"	White, Elisha	"
Miller, John	"	Warner, Henry	"
Pettecord, John	"	Waters, John	"
Reanny, Isaac	"	Wilson, Joseph	"
Russall, William	"	Fleming, James	"
Ricketts, Levering	"		

Danl. Schwarzauer,	Captain.	Curbey, James	Private
Benj. Rawlings,	Lieutenant.	Conn, Jacob	"
Joshua F. Batchelor,	Ensign.	Craddick, Joseph	"
Michael Waters,	1st Serg't.	Dorbecker, Adam	"
Arch. A. Watkins,	2d do.	Dawson, Thomas	"
John Beard,	3d do.	Donaldson, Aaron	"
John Snyder,	4th do.	Dowlan, Daniel	"
James Achlan,	1st Corp'l.	Danaker, John	"
Chas. A. Mattee,	3d do.	Desk, Thomas	"
Jas. Moberry,	4th do.	Ever, Abraham	"
Alexander, Elie	Private.	Fosler, George	"
Anderson, Archibald	"	Ferguson, George	"
Bilmeyer, Jacob	"	Fowler, Samuel	"
Buckingham, Thomas	"	Fleetwood, Benj.	"
Benner, John	"	Freberger, Henry	"
Burk, William	"	Gibbs, John	"
Black, Fredk.	"	Glaucer, Jacob	"
Black, Joseph	"	Gibbs, Nicholas	"
Boyce, Benjamin	"	Jarrett, John	"
Chilcoat, Charles	"	Johnson, Nicholas	"
Cunningham, George	"	Kinley, Edward	"
Capito, Peter	"	Lefler, George	"

Logan, Samuel	Private.	Riggins, Joseph	Private.
Loud, Baltzer	"	Reppart, George	"
Miller, Philip	"	Richardson, Edward	"
McDermitt, James	"	Redman, John	"
Mixter, Ezra	"	Salques, Coley	"
Morrison, James	"	Shatner, Jacob	"
Munn, John	"	Saunders, Thomas	"
Miller, John	"	Saunders, James	"
Mortimer, Thomas	"	Starr, George	"
McIntire, John	"	Tatcham, Daniel	"
Merritt, John	"	Tunis, Samuel	"
McLaughlin, John	"	Trucit, Robert	"
Nash, Ephraim	"	Torrenson, John	"
Poulston, John	"	Mark, Aaron	"
Parsons, Joseph	"	Walker, Benjamin	"
Pope, Elijah	"	Watson, John	"
Pennington, William	"	Webb, Perry	"
Robinson, Jesse	"	Hardman, John	Musician.
Robinson, Andrew	"	Cowhem, William	do.

Names of the Field and Staff and Company Officers, Non-Commissioned Officers and Privates of the thirty-ninth Regiment of the Maryland Militia, who served at North Point and Fort McHenry, 12th September, 1814—taken from the Muster Rolls on file in the Office of the Third Auditor of the Treasury of the United States.

BENJAMIN FOWLER, *Lieutenant Colonel.*
JACOB STEIGERS, *Major.*
GEORGE HENNICK, *Major.*
THOMAS BALTZELL, 1*st Lieutenant and Adjutant.*
OWEN DORSEY, 1*st Lieutenant and Pay Master.*
THOMAS MUMMY, 1*st Lieutenant and Qr. Master.*
HENRY HOWARD, *Surgeon.*
AMOS CORBIN, *Surgeon's Mate.*
JOSEPH BARCKLEY, *Sergeant Major.*
SAMUEL YOUNG, *Quarter Master's Sergeant.*

Archibald Dobbin, Captain.	James Smith	Serg't.
Thomas Cole, Lieutenant.	John H. Wilson,	do.
Robert Cummins, Ensign.	Joseph Sindorff,	Corporal.
Thomas Harwood, Serg't.	John Lynes,	do.
William Saukee, do.	Benj. Grammar,	do.

John Maxwell, Corp'l.	Knight, John	Private.
Barrows, Elijah	Private. Keirnan, Charles	"
Berry, James	" Light, John	"
Burnes, Timothy	" Leonard, Amassa	"
Baine, Andrew	" Lynch, Patrick	"
Britton, John	" McDonald, John	"
Baltzell, Lewis	" Meeks, William	"
Beck, John	" Marsh, John J.	"
Channel, James	" Messenger, Simpson	"
Carr, John	" Manning, Jesse	"
Chapman, John	" Mattox, Edward	"
Dempsey, John	" Mullenhoover, Josh.	"
Dinsmore, Patrick	" Norwood, John	"
Dorsey, Saml. J.	" Olcott, Joel	"
Drydon, William	" Phillips, John	"
Edgar, David	" Patterson, John	"
Fowler, James	" Patterson, George	"
Ford, Nicholas	" Porter, Jeptha	"
Fowler, Perry	" Roach, Thomas D.	"
Greenfield, Neilson	" Roe, Saml.	"
Gardenier, Wm.	" Roe, Charles	"
High, James	" Robinson, Jesse	"
Hewett, Michael	" Randle, Christopher	"
Hohn, Henry	" Silverthorn, Henry	"
Harwood, James	" Silance, Richard	"
Harris, Joseph	" Scipe, Michael	"
James, Singleton	" Thomas, Gabriel	"
Isett, Adam	" Thompson, John	"
Joy, Peter	" Whorley, Jonathan	"
Kilbourne, Saml.	" Wolf, George	"
Keplinger, Saml.	" Worthington, Nichs.	"

Thomas Warner, Captain.	Hope, Daniel	Private.
Benjamin Tevis, 1st Lieut.	Hone, Joseph	"
Thos. S. Williams, Ensign.	Hulstine, Michael	"
Horace H. Haden, Serg't.	Jackson, Archibald	"
James G. Hilton, do.	Linderman, William	"
William Hardy, Corporal.	Noah, Lowry	"
Adams, Soseph	Private. McPhail, Daniel	"
Armstrong, Joshua	" Merrican, John	"
Baker, Ernest	" McKnight, John	"
Butler, Moses	" McIohammer, John	"
Campbell, John	" Nabb, William	"
Curley, James	" Neagle, James	"
Desney, Benj.	" Oram, Lloyd	"
Dent, Walter	" Redeffer, Jacob	"
Downes, James	" Saddler, Joseph	"
Fenton, William	" Schaffer, Christian	"
Grant, Elijah	" Swiggett, Robert T.	"

Sutton, Solomon	Private.	Woodward, Abraham	Private.
Tyler, Levin	"	Ways, William	"
Todd, Lancelott	"	Weir, Lemuel	"

Thomas Watson, Captain.		Hay, David	Private.
William Woody, Lieutenant.		Hasley, Samuel	"
William Baltzell, Ensign.		Hiser John	"
Jacob Hoffman, Ser'gt.		Hunterman, Dedrick	"
James Wilson do.		Hemling, Anthony	"
John C. Snyder, Corporal.		Hamilton, John A.	"
John Wilson, do.		Hogner, John	"
Adrey, William	Private.	Hurmange, Peter	"
Adrey, Levin	"	Keiner, Melker	"
Anderson, William	"	Lyon, William	"
Brannen, William	"	Meriken, Joseph	"
Bodensick, Henry	"	McCutchen, George	"
Barkman, John	"	McNichalls, Isaac	"
Brown, John C.	"	McLean, Charles	"
Chalmers, John	"	Mass, Robert	"
Cooper, Samuel	"	Nichols, Samuel	"
Cole, Elsey	"	Smith, James	"
Deshorg, James	"	Spedden, Edward	"
Ewing, Samuel	"	Strike, William	"
Eichelberger, Samuel	"	Simpson, John D.	"
Fuss, John	"	Thompson, Bernard	"
Fleming, Frederick	"	Turpin, George	"
France, Thomas	"	Uhler, Henry	"
Gobright, William	"	Walker, Isaac	"
Grainger, Matthew	"	Worreil, John	"
Gutrow, James	"	Wilson, William	"

John D. Miller, Captain.		Clayton, Samuel	Private.
Erasmus Uhler, 1st Lieut.		Craxall, Charles	"
Jas. H. Vanarsdale, Ensign.		Dean, James	"
Daniel Hamer,	1st Serg't.	Hamilton, John	"
Ritson Browning,	2d do.	Ireland, Richard	"
Isaac Thomas,	3d do.	Kauffman, Daniel	"
Jacob Wolf, jr.,	4th do.	Knuff, Abraham	"
John Fisher,	1st Corp'l.	Kauffman, John	"
Spencer Coburn,	Drummer.	Krebbs, John	"
Stephen Pater,	Fifer.	Lepelticr, Francis	"
Amick, Daniel	Private.	Link, Henry	"
Amick, Jacob	"	Marr, Alexander	"
Bear, William	"	McMullen, Thomas	"
Brown, Christian	"	Perrine, Peter	"
Brown, Obed	"	Potee, Peter	"
Bates, Joseph	"	Shaves, Robert	"

Simpers, Benj. Private. Thrush, Nicholas Private.
Simmering, John " Vansant, John "
Simmering, Christian " Walter, Philip "
Sullivan, John " Weaver, Aquilla "
Smallwood, George "

Andw. E. Warner, Captain.* McKennion, James Private.
Peter Leary, Lieutenant. Matlock, John "
William Eckel, Ensign. Oram, Rezen "
Valentine Birely, 1st Serg't. Porter, William "
John Thomas, 2d do. Pawley, John "
John Garrett, 3d do. Ryan, George "
Eb'r. Pumphrey, 4th do. Roland, Joseph M. "
Boothe, Michael Private. Sederburgh, Trol "
Bare, John " Sumwalt, John "
Ballinger, Samuel " Swope, John "
Boggus, Robert " Smith, Andrew "
Dome, John " Sanders, Benjamin "
Degroff, Richard " Strebeck, William "
Evans, Joshua " Thompson, Stephen "
Green, John " Willey, John "
Garrey, Jeremiah " Williams, Owen "
Hawes, Frederick " White, Thomas "
Keilhoultz, Heery " Young, Samuel "
Levering, Peter " Young, John "

Henry Myers, Captain. Hix, William Private.
Samuel Wolf, 1st Lieutenant. Johnson, Charles "
George B. Sumwalt, Ensign. Johnson, James "
William Stansbury, 1st Serg't. Keyser, William "
John Skiles, 2d do. Kessler, Christian "
John Gibbs, 3d do. Knowlton, Silas "
Wm V. Morrison, 1st Corp'l. Kone, Daniel "
Wm. Lineberger, 2d do. Kirkland, David "
George W. Betts, 3d do. Munroe, James "
William Samuels, 3th do. Myers, John "
Appleby, Thomas Private. Mattocks, John "
Berry, Philip " Mass, Samuel "
Bausman, Joseph " Nussear, Joseph "
Camp, Joseph " Nussear, Jesse "
Correll, Nathan " Richardson, John "
Christielf, Henry " Robinson, John "
Cole, George " Robb, John "
Du Pois, Christopher " Ross, James "
Daily, William " Reinicker, Samuel "
Emory, Lott " Randolph, Thompson "
Haslett, James " Stall, Samuel "

*Mortally wounded.

Schorbb, Andrew	Private.	Wincett, Joseph	Private.
Scroggs, John	"	Whitelock, Charles	"
Welsh, George	"	Van Lear, Matthew	"

Jos. K. Stapleton, Captain.		Grinnell, William	Private.
William Myers, Lieutenant.		Grainer, William	"
Joseph Caldwell, Ensign.		Hammer, Daniel	"
Hugh Young,	Serg't.	Harkins, Giles	"
William G. Holland,	do.	Hagg, John	"
Charles Hogg,	do.	Hughes, William	"
H. B. Magruder,	do.	Jordon, John	"
James Leakins,	Corp'l.	Kitheart, William	"
Joseph Williams,	do.	Livers, Arnold	"
Charles Baltzell,	do.	Marrow, Isaac	"
Alexander Brady, Drummer.		Marrow, Hugh	"
Abbot, Francis A.	Private.	Milburn, Samuel	"
Abbott, Westley	"	Myers, Charles	"
Baltzell, Jacob	"	Oliver, John	"
Bradley, Lewis	"	Ogden, Jonathan	"
Banks, Daniel	"	Richards, J. C. (per proxy.)	
Bell, John H.	"	Thompson, John F.	"
Bowers, David	"	Redford, Jesse	"
Campbell, George W.	"	Robinson, John	"
Calhoun, Benjamin	"	Russell, William	"
Daily, Christian	"	Ruff, Henry	"
Daily, Elijah	"	Sadler, Joseph R.	"
Deal, Michael	"	Smith, Hugh	"
Donohoe, Patrick	"	Smithson, Archibald	"
Danse, Lepold	"	Sunderland, B.	"
Dooly, Rhoady	"	Sunderland, Richard	"
Dykes, Thomas	"	Tilyard, John	"
Dykes, John	"	Whitmarsh, John	"
File, John	"	Woods, Nicholas	"

William Roney, Captain.		Austin, Lawless	Private.
John Disney, Lieutenant.		Berrick, John	"
Henry Lusby, Ensign.		Bruce, Robert	"
George Sharrer,	1st Serg't.	Bundle, William	"
Peter Eisenbray,	2d do.	Bell, Ezekiel	"
Thomas Childs,	3d do.	Byard, Peter	"
John Hinds,	4th do.	Bull, Equilla	"
William Gable,	1st Corp'l.	Behoo, James	"
John Terry,	2d do.	Crangle, William	"
Richard Martin,	Musician.	Clopper, George	"
Aldnut, James	Private.	Clein, George	"
Aldhausen, Wm. J.	"	Cherry, Peter	"
Alexander, William	"	Crangle, James	"

Chambers, Philemon	Private	King, Jesse	Private
Carter, William	"	Lorr, Adam	"
Cook, Frederick	"	Lee, John	"
Coyle, David	"	Mass, Andrew	"
Curry, William	"	Martin, William	"
Cochran, William	"	Nicholis, David	"
Crangle, Henry	"	Ovaere, John	"
Donals, Isaac	"	Penn, George	"
Evans, John	"	Peters, William	"
Evans, Robert	"	Porter, Benjamin	"
Evans, Thomas	"	Pool, James	"
Forrester, John	"	Potee, Francis	"
Forrest, Nicholas	"	Ruff, Andrew	"
Fallier, George	"	Rees, John	"
Fisher, Martin	"	Shoeff, Isaac	"
French, Thomas	"	Sanders, Joseph	"
Forrest, Allen	"	Smithson, Thomas	"
Griffith, Stephen	"	Thompson, Samuel	"
Gable, John	"	Teplin, William	"
Hissey, Archibald	"	Thompson, Wm.	"
Hicks, John	"	Warner, Henry	"
Hollingsworth, Thos.	"	Williams, John	"
Higden, Ralph	"	Williams, John, jr.	"
Hyson, Nicholas	"	Young, William	"
Jackson, William	"	Zody, John	"
King, George	"		

Names of the Field and Staff and Company Officers, Non-Commissioned Officers and Privates of the fifty-first Regiment of Maryland Militia, who served at North Point and Fort McHenry, 12th September, 1814—taken from the Muster Rolls on file in the office of the Third Auditor of the Treasury of the United States:

HENRY AMEY, *Lieutenant Colonel.*
JOHN YOUNG, *First Major.*
JOHN MATTHEWS, *Second Major.*
THOS. TWEETING, *Adjutant and Lieutenant.*
OLIVER H. NEILSON, *Quarter Master.*
GEORGE WARNER, *Pay Master.*
RICHARD W. HALL, *Surgeon.*
JOHN ARNEST, *Surgeon's Mate.*
MICHAEL WARNER, *Quarter Master.*
JAMES JOHNSTON, *Sergeant Major.*

57

Jacob Deems, Captain.	Jones, John	Private.
Littleton Holland, Lieutenant,	Jones, Dorsey	"
Joseph Little, Ensign.	Irvine, Dan'l.	
Stephen Culverwell, 1st Serg't.	Krems, Reinhart	"
Ephraim Francis, 2d do.	Lambert, John	"
Alfred Crump, 3d do.	McPherson, John	"
Valentine Dushane, 4th do.	Miller, Andrew	"
Levi Crossgrove, 1st Corp'l.	May, Jonas	"
Benjamin Comegys, 2d do.	Martin, Thomas	"
William Faithful, 3d do.	McEvoy, James	"
William Wright, 4th do.	McCarthy, Alex.	"
Allcock, William Private.	McCrea, Robert	"
Briggs, Richard "	Noone, John	"
Beck, John "	Perrigoy, James	"
Bailor, John "	Pell, Thomas	"
Bennett, John "	Parlett, Thomas	"
Brown, Joseph "	Reed, Joshua	"
Chamberlain, Philip "	Roberts, Thomas	"
Cutcher, Samuel "	Reed, Samuel	"
Crussen, Francis "	Reddy, William	"
Cooper, Ambrose "	Reed, Caleb	"
Dougherty, Neal "	Rea, William	"
Donovan, Jeremiah "	Shea, Harvey	"
Dodge, Alpheus "	Smithson, Nathan	"
Davids, John "	Scarf, William	"
Duvall, Nathan "	Stevenson, John	"
Dillon, David "	Sellers, John	"
Dillman, Peter "	Shipley, Zachariah	"
Eggleston, Benjamin "	Starr, James	"
Eggleston, Joseph "	Swern, William	"
Elliott, Thomas "	Shaeffer, Joseph	"
Farrell, Thomas "	Somers, John	"
Fort, Joshua "	Sanders, Edward	"
French, William "	Sowerwein, Daniel	"
Garrett, Thomas "	Tambo, David	"
Giles, Joseph "	Thompson, John	"
Griffin, Martin "	Warrington, John	"
Gattig, Jacob "	Williams, Richard	"
Gassaway, John "	Winters, Henry	"
Hogg, James "	West, Elijah	"
Harper, John "	Wheeler, Benj.	"
Hackney, William "	Winn, William	"
Henderson, Robt. "	Walter, Benj.	"
Hinton, James "	Whitney, Simon	"
Henry, Francis "	Whittington, Benj.	"
Henry, Hugh "	Yuncet, Leonard	"
Jones, Uriah "	Zimmerman, Jacob	"

William Chalmers, Captain.	Edward Kelly,	Serg't.
John T. Wallace, Lieutenant.	Stephen Sroud,	do.
John Kirby, Ensign.	Alex. Chambers,	do.

58

Robert McAllister, Serg't.	Keplinger, Michael	Private.
Joseph Lawrence, Corp'l.	Kinley, Daniel	"
Jacob Foss, do.	Kidd, John	"
James Darling, do.	Kelner, George	"
George Oppold, do.	Kidd, Joshua	"
Allen, John Private	Kerwell, Samuel	"
Armitage, William "	McCaully, Arthur	"
Allen, Henry "	McCormack, John	"
Brian, Thomas "	Moor, Thomas	"
Bain, James "	Mumma, Jacob	"
Bare, Henry "	McDonald, Charles	"
Bradley, James "	Mildews, Nathan	"
Patton, Robert "	Myers, John	"
Bromwell, Jacob "	Mitchell, John	"
Batchela, William "	McCormock, Jno. jr.	"
Barton, Joshua "	Moffit, John	"
Berry, Sam'l. "	Neal, John	"
Casey, Christopher "	Overhoff, Frederick	"
Clark, Joseph "	Parsons, Thomas	"
Chambers, Joseph "	Riley, William	"
Delcher, Thomas "	Randall, William	"
Dougherty, John "	Sprinkle, Daniel	"
Duncan, John "	Schunk, Jacob	"
Deaver, Thomas "	Sheldon, James } Bros.	"
Dougherty, Charles "	Sheldon, John }	
Emerling, Christian "	Sterling, William	"
Ellis, William "	Stevenson, Alex.	"
Fletcher, William "	Thrush, John	"
Fletcher, James "	Tidings, Rinaldo	"
Ingelbrits, Daniel "	Taylor, John	"
Gibbons, Thomas "	Thrailkill, George	"
Gordon, James "	Wilson, James	"
Graham, James "	Wood, Isaac	"
Grady, Anthony "	White, Thomas	"
Gosling, Joshua "	William, Abraham R.	"
Gamble, Alexander "	White, Stephen	"
Gladson, Michael "	Welslager, George	"
Hollbrooks, John "	Wilson, Samuel	"
Hayes, Abraham "	Wright, Thomas	"
Holland, Thomas "	Warner, John	"
Harker, William "	Wilson, Greenbury	"
Hatton, Joshua "	Yeager, John	"
Hooker, Jesse "		

John H. Rogers, Captain.	James Scantling,	Private.
Peter Hedges, Lieutenant.	Richard Helms, Fifer.	
Charles Brown, Ensign.	William Morrow, Drummer.	
William Shipley, Private.	Abbey, Jacob	Private.
Hartman Cuppold, "	Allen, John	"
Jacob Shultz, 1st Serg't	Alfred, James	"

Abey, Joseph	Private.	Kesler, John	Private.
Abel, Stanfield	"	Keem, Thomas W.	"
Brown, John	"	Kurtz, Henry	"
Barrow, James B.	"	Layman, Nicholas	"
Beemer, Henry	"	Love, James	"
Berrige, Robert	"	May, Thomas	"
Busick, John	"	Marker, John	"
Boyd, William	"	Mahoney, Elisha	"
Butcher, Joseph	"	McArdel, Henry	"
Busey, Samuel	"	Miller, John	"
Bushey, George	"	Mills, Henry	"
Boyer, John	"	Martin, Mordecai	"
Blunt, John	"	Neppod, Jacob	"
Camden, James	"	Nicholson, Thomas	"
Converse, Elijah	"	Night, John	"
Cramer, William	"	Patterson, Nathan,	Serg't.
Coats, Searson	"	Paterson, Thomas	Private.
Cowley, Edward	"	Perigo, Jehu	"
Carter, William	"	Roberts, John	"
Collins, Josias	"	Rusk, David L.	"
Chapman, Richard	"	Randall, Jesse	"
Dyer, Ignatius	"	Reese, William	"
Edler, John	"	Sheppard, David	"
Fletcher, Thomas,	"	Sanders, John	"
Foreman, Francis	"	Sawner, George	"
Fowble, Peter, Serg't.		Schroyer, Daniel	"
Feguet, Dominick, Corp'l.		Shoat, Abraham	"
Fetle, Joseph	Private.	Scoby, John	"
Fitzgerald, Austin	"	Sawner, John	"
Fowble, Peter, jr.	"	Seemon, Jacob	"
Gamble, Robert	"	Shannon, John	"
Gamble, Stephen	"	Shields, James	"
Goodwin, Jacob	"	Taylor, Samuel	"
Gall, Jacob	"	Towson, John	"
Hanes, David	"	Towson, Thomas	"
Howard Perry	"	Taylor, William	"
Halsy, Michael	"	Wright, William E.	"
Holmes, Joseph	"	Wise, John	"
Holmes, Thomas	"	Wheaton, Cloudsbury	"
Hollin, John, Corp'l.		Weedon, Arthur	"
Johnson, Elijah	Private.	Young, John	"

Michael Haubert, Captain. James Lambdon, Corp'l.
Foster Maynard, Lieutenant. David Brand, do.
John Carroll, Ensign. John Thomas, do.
George Milliman, Serg't. Jacob G. Cromwell, do.
John Davis, do. Allen, Andrew Private.
Ignatius Boarman, do. Allen, David "
John Winstanly, do. Able, Christian "

Broughton, Noah	Private.	Laivett, Peter	Private.
Brown, Jacob S.	"	Logan, Joseph	"
Bard, Dan'l.	"	McMechan, Sam'l.	"
Barber, James	"	McGloshen, Robt.	"
Boyle, William	"	Miller, Jacob	"
Blotner, Matthias	"	Mathias, Nicholas	"
Bushy, Jacob	"	Moore, John	"
Barge, William	"	Morgan, William	"
Bond, Benj.	"	Mathias, John	"
Bell, Cornelius	"	McDonoh, Peter	"
Cox, Kempson	"	McLaughlin, Francis	"
Clements, Robert H.	"	Miller, Thomas	"
Clever, Derick	"	McDonon, Patrick	"
Cook, Elisha	"	Morton, William	"
Caughy, Patrick	"	Malony, Owen	"
Cohagan, Joshua	"	Naskey, John	"
Crump, George	"	Nelms, J. B.	"
Callahan, Charles	"	Peach, Philip	"
Callahan, Peter	"	Parker, George	"
Duncan, Christian	"	Rily, Edward	"
Downs, Isaiah	"	Robinson, Abraham	"
Funk, Jacob	"	Rutter, John	"
Ford, John	"	Rosensteel Henry	"
Flee, Christian	"	Richardson, George	"
Griffin, Robt.	"	Ring, George	"
Grove, Jacob	"	Smitson, William	"
Geese, George	"	Siddler, Benj.	"
Griffith, John H.	"	Stall, Joseph	"
Gray, Zachariah	"	Sisser, Martin	"
Griffin, Nathan	"	Steiger, Tobias	"
Gill, John	"	Spear, John	"
Henderson, Zachariah	"	Stewart, Charles	"
Hanks, Lewis	"	Thornton, Edward	"
Hausman, Henry]	"	Thomas, Isaac	"
Holland, John	"	Triggle, Dorsey	"
Henderson, Peter	"	Thompson, Elias	"
Holliday, William	"	Thompson, Alex.	"
Henderson, David	"	Vallean, Henry	"
Hissey, Archibald	"	Ward, James	"
Harbison, Robt.	"	Ward, Edward	"
Hissey, Caleb	"	Weller, Martin	"
Hyson, Jacob	"	Weller, George	"
Henderson, Benj.	"	Wright, Abraham	"
Johnston, Abijah	"	Warring, E. R.	"
Joice, Aaron	"	Whelan, James	"
Jones, Griffin	"	Williams, Charles	"
Kauffman, Jonathan	"	Whelan, George	"
Killiam, James	"	Zorn, John	"
Klunk, Peter	"		

John Stewart, Captain.	Kelly, James	Private.
Jeremiah Boyd, 2d Lieut.	Lucas, James	"
John Hildt, Ensign.	Magarity, John	"
Jno. F. Utt, Serg't.	McPherson, John	"
Marshall Mask, do.	McCanna, William	"
George Waile, do.	Myers, Robert	"
Joseph Foss, do.	Mix, Lewis	"
Sam'l Samuels, Corp'l.	McDonald, James	"
Dan'l Foss, do.	McCauley, James	"
David Thompson, do.	McDonald, Thomas	"
James Smith, do.	McKim, William	"
All, William, Private.	McKearney, John	"
Addison, Isaac "	Maguire, Michael	"
Armitage, John "	McDermit, Stephen	"
Broughton, Isaac "	McDonald, John	"
Bameyalo, Nath'l. "	Micholson, Christopher	"
Bucher, Charles "	O'Brien, Patrick	"
Bates, Jacob "	Oneil, Joseph	"
Blaney, Daniel "	O'Harro, Arthur	"
Baxter, James "	Purnell, Rich'd.	"
Buchanan, Edw'd "	Pilgrim, Nath'l.	"
Conklin, Elijah "	Pastorias, Sam'l.	"
Cheny, Edw'd. "	Philips, Charles	"
Curlett, Robert "	Patterson, Andrew	"
Clark, Nath'l. "	Parker, Thomas	"
Carr, Teague "	Ross, Solomon	"
Conly, Michael "	Ridgely, Davidge	"
Coleman, Alex. "	Ramsay, William	"
Corwine, Jehu "	Rourk, Peter	"
Carty, Josiah "	Slack, James	"
Downing, Howell "	Simpson, Sam'l.	"
Dykes, James "	Scaff, George	"
Ellis, John "	Schrœder, George	"
Essender, Thomas "	Smith, Jacob	"
Eich, Philip "	Sutherland, Dan'l.	"
Emerson, James "	Spears, James	"
Feishel, Anthony "	Sewell, Reuben	"
Ford, Stephen "	Sweetzer, John	"
Gawthrop, Thomas "	Stocker, Elijah	"
Gillen, Lakey "	Senseny, Jacob	"
Gordon, Joseph "	Shields, William	"
Gosmann, James "	Thompson, John	"
Holmes, James "	Taylor, Aquila	"
Hinneman, William "	Thompson, William	"
Heneker, Peter "	Townsend, Perry	"
Hanawalt, Jacob "	Townsend, James	"
Joice, Jesse "	Toy, Joseph	"
Iles, Henry "	Wax, Henry	"
Jag, Sam'l. "	Walker, Peter	"
Kalbfus, Dan'l. Md. Serg't.	Whitelock, John	"

James Faster, Captain.
John Simons, Lieut.
George Shoemaker, Ensign.
Charles Willbee, 1st Serg't
George W. Evans, 2d do.
Joseph Legard, 3d do.
Edward Speake, 4th do.
Howell Powell, 1st Corp'l.
Hugh R. Marshall, 2d do.
John Wolverton, 3d do.
Sterling Thomas, 4th do.
Aiken, William, Private.
Appleby, John "
Britt, Severn "
Bradley, William "
Brown, John E. "
Baloon, Pasquel "
Burch, George "
Carter, Clement "
Clark, Mills "
Carson, Robert "
Curtain, James "
Compton, John "
Dureling, John T. "
Erickson, Thomas "
Evans, Jeremiah "
Freer, Peter "
Fletcher, John "
Green, Armistead "
Griffin, George "
Griffis, Edward "
Galagher, Hugh "
Gibbons, John "
Gardner, Henry "
Groover, Charles "
Hayes, William "
Hall, James J. "
Harman, Daniel H. "

Hall, Josiah Private.
Halfpenny, John "
Johnson, William "
Jones, John "
Jenkins, Jason "
Joice, William "
Kalbfus, William "
Lancaster, Enoch "
Lewis, Willoughby "
McCormick, James "
McElderry, John "
McElderry, Thomas "
Mathews, Patrick "
Manly, James "
Mortimer, John "
Nelson, Robert "
Pilcher, Warner "
Pameroy, Ralph "
Plains, George "
Phelps, Gardner "
Robinson, William "
Remmy, Richard "
Rinehart, David "
Ratiken, John "
Scott, John L. "
Solomon, Samuel "
Sweetman, Willis "
Swain, John "
Severson, Thomas "
Thompson, Alex., jr. "
Trill, Samuel "
Watters, Isaac "
Ware, John "
Ward, James "
Weaver, Henry "
Walter, William "
Widderfeld, William "

Michael Peters, Captain.
Robert H. J. Stewart, Lieut.
Francis Murray, Ensign.
John Brannon, 1st Serg't.
William Crist, 2d do.
William Edwards, 3d do.
Abra'm Edwards, 4th do.
Martin Eichelberger, 2d Cor.
James Larew, 3d do.
Joshua C. Atkinson, 4th do.

James Hull, Musician.
Darius Wheeler, do.
Atmos, William H. Private
Alford, John "
Burland, James "
Barton, William "
Bunting, John "
Benson, John "
Brawner, Daniel "
Booth, Addison "

Cox, Edward	Private.	Matchett, Richard J.	Private.
Carson, Morgan	"	Meed, Isaiah	"
Chambers, Robert	"	Maydwell, James	"
Chattles, Samuel	"	Miller, Charles	"
Cherry, Dominick	"	McDonald, John	"
Church, John	"	Myers, Barnard	"
Carson, David	"	McCormick, Thomas	"
Corbin, Henry	"	McCullough, James	"
Ditman, John	"	Newton, John	"
Dougherty, Philip	"	Peters, Adam	"
Elmore, James	"	Price, Walter	"
Enson, William	"	Parr, David	"
Elliott, John	"	Potut, Jesse	"
Fowler, Isaac D.	"	Parr, Elisha	"
Ford, Thomas	"	Pindell, John	"
Frazier, William	"	Richardson, John	"
Frick, Christian	"	Slemmer, Christian	"
Fous, Jacob	"	Schunck, Philip	"
Fawsbeuner, Andrew	"	Schunck, John	"
Frick, William	"	Sindell, John	"
Grooms, William	"	Sindell, Thomas	"
Gilbert, David	"	Sindell, Joshua	"
Gray, Allen	"	Spear, William	"
Greggs, Elbeu	"	Strider, John	"
Gairy, William G.	"	Stubbins, Thomas	"
Hatton, John	"	Sinton, Joseph	"
Henegar, Frederick	"	Summerville, John	"
Holtz, Peter	"	Smith, John	"
Hiss, Jacob	"	Srimard, John	"
Johnson, Harman	"	Stansbury, Richard	"
Jeremiah, John	"	Swann, Joshua	"
Jordan, George	"	Till, William	"
Johnson, David	"	Tuts, George	"
Kelso, Thomas	"	Thornburgh, James C.	"
Kent, John	"	Ward, John D.	"
Kite, James	"	Wilson, James	"
Lougellee, Lewis	"	Williams, Benjamin	"
Miller, John	"	Willingham, James	"
Mettee, Joseph	"	Williams, Joseph	"
McKubbin, Samuel	"	Way, Frederick	"
McNier, William	"	Zerne, Christian	"
Moore, Joshua	"		

Andrew Smith, Captain.		Peter Eichelberger, Serg't.	
Samuel Leath, Lieutenant.		David D. Smith,	Corp'l.
Henry Timanus, Ensign.		Wm. B. Reynolds,	do.
William L. Crossmore, Serg't.		Mathias Shrote,	do.
John Henshaw,	do.	Richard Snyder,	do.
Joshua Shipley,	do.	Adams, Thomas	Private.

Anderson, Joseph	Private.	Koutz, George	Private.
Arms, Austin	"	Linebargar, Samuel	"
Allman, Henry	"	Lindenburger, John C.	"
Byus, Joseph	"	Luster, Shipley	"
Barme, John	"	Liams, Jeremiah	"
Brooks, Robert	"	Lloyd, William	"
Bagwell, Elie	"	Lewis, John	"
Baum, Archibald	"	Mahoney, Mathias	"
Baker, Jacob	"	Mosel, John	"
Bear, Joseph	"	McCuller, James	"
Billson, Joseph	"	Marshall, Thomas	"
Battimore, Thomas	"	Mincher, Joseph	"
Belt, George	"	Mincher, John	"
Curty, Clowdsbury	"	McGrok, Andrew	"
Chenoeth, Joshua	"	McNulty, Israel	"
Chamberlaine, James	"	Morgan, William	"
Cook, Joseph	"	McGuire, John	"
Dennis, John	"	Miller, Adam	"
Downey, Edmund	"	Murphy, Basil	"
Davis, Benjamin	"	McCurley, Felix	"
Dooghman, Peter	"	Nicholson, Thomas	"
Dumiste, George	"	Nelson, Richard	"
Detro, Levi	"	Nelson, Nathaniel	"
Damute, Peter	"	Newcummer, John	"
Dawes, Richard	"	Naylor, George	"
Foy, Frederick	"	Patterson, John	"
Ford, Walter	"	Piper, Philip	"
Gibbs, John	"	Pepple, Peter	"
Griffin, Charles K.	"	Peirce, Samuel	"
Grubb, William	"	Peck, Jacob	"
Gombey, George	"	Peirce, Elias	"
Guest, Richard	"	Penn, John	"
Gold, John	"	Rogers, John	"
Garrett, John	"	Robinson, William	"
Gray, Callender	"	Randle, Jacob	"
Hogner, William	"	Righter, George	"
High, David	"	Rogers, Roland	"
Hobbs, William	"	Rosensteel, William	"
Hart, Joseph	"	Rusk, Paul	"
Hussey, Isaac	"	Smith, William	"
Hassaid, Ralph	"	Scavon, William	"
Harrison, Stephen	"	Stembler, John	"
Haftey, Jacob	"	Smith, Elie	"
Harbaugh, Daniel	"	Smith, Adam	"
Hugues, Aquila	"	Stinchcomb, Victor	"
Hall, James	"	Steigers, George	"
Ichler, John	"	Sanders, Humphrey	"
Kemberly, Michael	"	Stricke, Nicholas	"
Keys, William	"	Shipley, William	"
Krouse, Jacob	"	Sanderson, Francis	"
Kitheart, Robert	"	Shrote, Mathias, jr.	"

Steigers, John	Private.	Weaver, Joseph	Private.
Taylor, Philip	"	Whitoford, David	"
Trowbridge, Reuben	"	Walter, Joseph A.	"
Vermillion, Joseph	"	Williamson, Peregrine	"
Whirrett, Thomas	"	Webb, Frederick	"
Wigley, Edward	"	Warfield, Basil H.	"
Wilson, Otho	"	Yeamon, Royal	"

Names of officers and enlisted men of Capt. Wm. H. Addison's Company of Sea Fencibles, stationed at Fort McHenry, Md., September and October, 1814, as per muster roll for said period.

Wm H. Addison, Capt.		Day, Cornelious	Private.
Caleb P. Robenson, 2d Lieut.		Dalton, Edward	"
George McNeir,	3d do.	Eliott, Benjamin	"
John Tyler, Boatswain.		Evins, David	"
Zacheous Stoker, Gunner.		Freeman, Wm.	"
James L. Stevens,	do.	Gardner, Samuel	"
Andrew H. Fife,	do.	George, Ezekiel	"
Patrick Handlin,	do.	George, James	"
James Childs,	do.	Gordon, John	"
Wm Peregoy,	do.	Griffiths, Thos. B.	"
Wm. Hanson, Quarter Gunner.		Hutton, Sam'l	"
James Dawson,	do.	Hollings, John	"
Sa m'l McDonald,	do.	Harris, John	"
Sam'l Jordan,	do.	Hambly, James	"
John Swift,	do.	Hadley, Joseph	"
John McCracken,	do.	Hands, Ephram	"
Alford, Thomas	Private.	Hands, Nicholas	"
Askew, Charles	"	Hane, Jacob, jr.	"
Alford, Jacob	"	Hamilton, John	"
Andrews, John	"	Ing, John	"
Barnhart, Henry	"	Izer, Joshua	"
Barall, Lewis	"	Keplinger, George	"
Belott, Wm.	"	Lacey, Wm	"
Bongers, Peter C.	"	Limner, Taurance	"
Bebee, Edward	"	Mackey, Robert	"
Cook, Samuel	"	McDowel, Thos.	"
Crocken, James	"	Mestler, Coonrod	"
Carr, George	"	McCoy, Alexander	"
Cary, Dennis	"	Miles, John	"
Cooper, Hesekiah	"	McComas, Charles	"
Clark, James M	"	Morgan, John	"
Curtis, John	"	Newit, Edward	"
Caffery, John R.	"	Nary, Michael	"

Peters, Wm.	Private.	Scott, Joseph	Private.
Rook, John	"	Spicer, Joseph	"
Rick, John	"	Trimble, John	"
Redman, James	"	Vinyard, James	"
Redman, Joshua	"	Walsh, Moses	"
Shartle, Henry	"	Westwood, Thos.	"
Sadler, Augustus	"	Wilson, Charles	"
Smith, Wm.	"	Williams, Richard	"
Shryark, Samuel	"	Wood, Leven W.	"
Scott, Richard	"	Wallace, James	"
Skipper, David	"	White, Wm. W.	"
Sinton, Francis	"	Williams, Wm.	"
Stimpson, Stephen	"	Warrick, John	"
Smithson, Luther	"	Stepenson, John, Servant.	
Simons, James	"	Potter, Thos.	"
Sheliey, Michael	"	Williams, Job	"

Names of officers and enlisted men of a Company of Sea Fencibles, commanded by Capt. M. Simmones Bunbury, as given on muster roll for July and August, 1814. Muster roll for September and October, 1814, not on file in this office.

M. S. Bunbury, Captain.		Bailey, Esma	Private.
Gregory Foy,	1st Lieut.	Cowdery, Isaac	"
Gerard Gorsuch,	2d do.	Conrad, John	"
James Lawrenson, Boatswain.		Craig, John	"
George Bussel,	Gunner.	Cooper, John	"
John Wood,	do.	Connally, John	"
Joseph P. White,	do.	Dear, Isaac	"
John Coomes,	do.	Drear, Joseph	"
John Valiant,	do.	Devou, I. William	"
Hugh Crea,	do.	Evans, Patrick	"
William Jones,	Qr. Gunner.	Edmunds, Abijah	"
Thomas Broom,	do.	Forsey, P. Elias	"
Peter Young,	do.	Fletcher, John	"
Benjamin White,	do.	Frederick, Paul	"
George C. Wilson,	do.	Goodmanson, Peter	"
Noah Higby,	do.	Green, Robert	"
Barbine Charles	Private.	Green, John	"
Brinkman, John	"	Gibson, Thomas	"
Brown, John, 1st	Private.	Green, Anthony	"
Brown, John, 2d	do.	Hash, Peter	"
Blunt, Joseph	Private.	Hall, Joseph	"
Blare, Charles	"	Hanes, James	"
Bennett, Freeman	"	Hayes, Adam	"

Henry, John	Private.	Robertson, Thomas	Private.
Jackson, John	"	Sterrett, Robert	"
Koog, Martin	"	Smith, Alexander	"
Kincaid, Myers	"	Shearman, I. Lewis	"
Livres, G William	"	Scracklin, Lewis	"
Luley, Charles	"	Stephens, Timothy	"
Manson, Henry	"	Sparks, William	"
Meeks, P. James	"	Thompson, Rich'd	"
Marshall, Elias	"	Travlot, John	"
McKnight, Lewis	"	Warfield, George	"
Montgomery, Arch'd.	"	Welsh, Pierce	"
Morris George	"	Wilson, William	"
Oram, John	"	Williams, James, 2d	"
Page, Jenkin	"	White, Charles	"
Patterson, William	"	Welsh, John	"
Ross, S. Samuel	"	Thomas Hall,	Servant.
Rogers, Joseph	"	Timothy Wailino,	do.
Richardson, William	"	Sam'l Herd	do.

—   —

Names of officers and enlisted men of Captain Frederick Evans' Company, Corps artillery, stationed at Fort McHenry, Md., September and October, 1814, as per Muster Roll for said period.

Frederick Evans, Captain.		Eli West	Artificer.
George Reardon, 3d Lieut.		James McCatlin,	do.
Edward Dawes,	do.	Joshua Clark,	do.
William Stewart, H. S. M.		John Brady,	do.
Thomas Morgan,	Serg't..	Patrick Roney,	do.
John Luckett,	do.	Austin, David	Private.
Joseph Lyon,	do.	Achy, Peter	"
Isaac H. Gorham,	do.	Allison, James	"
John H. Elkins, Corporal.		Ackley, David	"
Spedden Wilson,	do.	Bentley, Jonas	"
Dennis Sweeney,	do.	Bickford, Benjamin S. C.	"
Philip Boiala,	do.	Bush, Mark	"
Owen Allen,	do.	Body, Peter	"
Frederick Hosford, do.		Bagill, John	"
John Tillet,	Musician.	Brigdell, Daniel	"
Samuel Lyon,	do.	Cross, Horatio	"
William Harriss,	do.	Crumpton, John	"
George Shellenberg, do.		Craig, Benjamin	"
John Daniels,	Artificer.	Coloon, John	"
George Pope,	do.	Cadle, William	"
George Garring,	do.	Clark, George	"

Eagleston, Benjamin	Private.	Smith, Isaac	Private.
Eldridge, Levi	"	Sherer, Elias	"
Edwards, Jerret	"	Sweeney, Benjamin	"
Gerring, Daniel	"	Sweeney, John	"
Guthrow, Joseph	"	Thompson, Mathew	"
Govrele, Andrew	"	Shaffer, Henry	"
Gray, William	"	Wincett, Joseph	"
Hill, Richard S.	"	Walker, Fielder	"
Hamilton, David	"	Whitson, George R.	"
Holmes, John	"	Miller, Peter	"
Herron, John	"	Parsons, Samuel	"
Jackson, Samuel	"	Williams, Lancelot	"
Jackson, Robert	"	Bower, Samuel	"
Johnson, William	"	Davis, John	"
Kelly, Patrick	"	McCoy, Hugh	"
Knight, Elitus	"	Regard, Caleb	"
Levare, Joseph	"	Bowen, John	"
Lyon, John	"	Doll, John	"
Laughlin, James	"	Brown, Stephen	"
Morey, Jonathan	"	Williams, George	"
Manning, Dennis	"	Smith, Charles	"
Murphy, Josiah	"	Dement, Edward	"
McAna, George	"	Bozen, Henry	"
McCrae, Archbd.	"	Hemmenway, John	"
Nowland, Peter	"	Murray, John	"
O'Neal, John	"	Jones, William	"
O'Connor, John	"	William ———,	Servant
Powell, William	"	Philip Cypress,	do.
Quinn, Edward	"	Barney Hamilton,	do.
Reamos, Emanuel	"	Henry Bordley,	do.
Reynolds, Connor	"	William Cross,	do.
Rittallack, Simon	"	Elias Cross,	do.
Russell, Dewey	"	Anthenas Catesto,	do.
Peters, Conrad	"	Willes ———,	do.
Smith, William	"		

DEFENSE OF BALTIMORE.

RESOLVES OF THE CITIZENS IN TOWN MEETING, PARTICULARS RELATING TO THE BATTLE, OFFICIAL CORRESPONDENCE, AND HONORABLE DISCHARGE OF THE TROOPS.

From Niles' Register.

BALTIMORE, August 27, 1813.

BY THE COMMITTEE ON VIGILANCE AND SAFETY.

Whereas the commanding officer has required the aid of the citizens in the erection of works for the defense of the city, and the committee of vigilance and safety having full confidence in the patriotism of their fellow citizens, have agreed on the following organization, for the purpose of complying with the request of the major general.

The inhabitants of the city and precincts are called on to deposit at the court-house in the third ward, centre market in the fifth ward, market house Fell's Point, Riding-school in the seventh ward, or take with them to the place required, all wheel-barrows, pick-axes, spades and shovels that they can procure.

That the city and precincts be divided into four sections, the first section to consist of the eastern precincts and the eighth ward, the second to comprise the 5th, 6th and 7th wards, the third to comprise the 2d, 3d and 4th wards, and the fourth to comprise the 1st ward and western precincts.

That the exempts from military and the free people of color of the first district, consisting of the 8th ward and eastern precincts, assemble to-morrow, Sunday morning, at 6 o'clock, at Hampstead-hill with provisions for the day, and that Arthur Mitchell, Daniel Conn, Henry Pennington, John Chalmers, William Starr, Thomas Weary, Henry Harwood and Philip Cornmiller be charged with their superintendence during the day.

That those of the second district, comprising the 5th, 6th and 7th wards, assemble at Myer Garden, on Monday morning at 6 o'clock under the superintendence of William Parks, Captain Watts, Ludwig Herring, William Ross, William Carman, Daniel Howland, Caleb Earnest and James Hutton.

That those of the third district, comprising the second, third and fourth wards, assemble at Washington Square, on *Tuesday morning*, at six o'clock, under the superintendence of Frederick Leypold, William M'Cleary, John McKim, jr., Henry Schroeder, Alexander M'Donald, Eli Hewitt, Peter Gold and Alexander Russell.

That those of the fourth district, comprising the 1st ward and western precincts, assemble at the intersection of Eutaw and Market streets, on Wednesday morning at 6 o'clock under the superintendence of William W. Taylor, William Jessop, Edward Harris, George Decker, William Harkins, Isaac Philips, William Jones and John Hignet.

The owners of the slaves are requested to send them to work on the days assigned in the several districts.

Such of our patriotic fellow citizens of the county or elsewhere, as are disposed to aid in the common defence, are invited to partake in the duties now required on such of the days as may be most convient to them.

(Signed)   EDWARD JOHNSON, Chairman.
THEODORE BLAND, Secretary.

BALTIMORE.

At the recommendation of the Committee of Vigilance and Safety, the people commenced their labors to fortify the city, on Sunday the 27th ult. The work done demonstrates their power and zeal, to the astonishment of all who behold it. *Baltimore* has long been remarkable for the patriotism and liberal spirit of her citizens; and her high character for these qualities is fully maintained by the free offering of *men* and *money* for the purposes of defence. In the meantime, volunteers and militia from the adjacent parts of *Maryland*, *Pennsylvania* and *Virginia*, have flocked in to our aid We are restrained, by the request of the Committee of Vigilance, from mentioning any particular; but the honorable record shall yet be made. We restrain the desire to notice these things *because* enjoined by the committee; for we are very sure the enemy is apprised of almost every thing that is transacted here; but he has learnt nothing to our discredit. The means of defence have given confidence to the people, many families who had left the city have returned; nothing is relaxed; every thing goes on as though an attack were immediately expected, but with the exception of performing their military duties, the people have their usual composure and quiet. To our brethren who have flown to our assistance, we are greatly indebted, as well for the decorum of their conduct in the city, as their patriotism in coming to the camp. The sudden collection of so many people, of all classes and conditions, might have been expected to create much confusion and disorder; but no event has yet occurred, that we have heard of, which can sully the character of an *individual* soldier; and the city is as quiet, (the sound of the drum, or the rattling of wagons pertaining to the different corps, excepted) as ever it was. This tribute is due to the *gentlemen* associated to repulse the enemy. Major General *Smith*, of the Maryland militia (of Mud Fort memory) commands the troops collected specially for the defence of *Baltimore*. Brigadier General *Winder* has under him the forces belonging to his military district. He is now here, and the whole is acting in concert.

A WHOPPER.

BALTIMORE.—The following, from "*his majesty's* printing office at Bermuda" as the article is headed, is the queerest and most lying account of the late attack upon Baltimore that we have yet seen, some "domestic manufactures" excepted:

"*Sept.* 23.—It appears from report, that after destroying Washington and taking possession of Alexandria, the small body of brave men under General Ross made an attack on Baltimore; the enemy had sunk the vessels, and but two or three small craft with bombs could approach: *they succeeded, however, in driving the Americans from the fort;* having to contend with a very superior force, eventually retired, as the occupation of the town, *which might have been gained*, would be a poor compensation for the sacrifice of many valuable lives."

ATTACK UPON BALTIMORE.

To detail, with reasonable accuracy, the minutiæ of the events that have happened at *Baltimore* since Sunday morning, the 11th inst., when the enemy made his appearance, to the time of his departure on the 15th, is not easily done: and we shall endeavor to give a succinct narration of the proceedings, with a steady eye to the truth of each matter referred to; avoiding, nevertheless, every thing that may tend to increase the information of the incendiary foe, as to our means of resources. Hence an account of our troops or works will not be expected. Sufficient is it to say, that the same force would make much less impression now than it did, or could have done, at the time of attack.

After the affair at Bladensburg and capture of Washington, an attack upon this city was confidently expected. Indeed, General *Ross* had fixed upon it for his *winter quarters;* and boasted, that with the force he had, he would go where he pleased through Maryland. Thus forewarned, considerable additions were made to the defences of the place—some of the troops of Gen. *Winder's* command were collected—*Rodgers* and *Perry* were here; and a good many noble volunteers flocked in from the adjacent parts of our own state and from *Virginia* and *Pennsylvania*. The Baltimore brigade was taken *en masse* into the service of the United States; and the whole submitted to the direction of Major General *Smith*, of the Maryland militia.

On Saturday, the 10th inst., we had information that the enemy was ascending the bay, and on Sunday morning his ships were seen at the mouth of our river, the Patapsco, in number from 40 to 50.—Some of his vessels entered the river, while others proceeded to *North Point*, (at the mouth of the Patapsco), distant 12 miles from the city, and commenced the debarkation of their troops in the night, which was finished early next morning. In the mean time the frigates, bomb ketches, and small vessels approached and ranged themselves in a formidable line to cannonade the fort, and the town.—The frigates were lightened before they entered the river—and the ships of line lay off North Point, to overawe us and protect the whole force.

The force that landed consisted of about 9,000 men—viz.: 5,000 soldiers, 2,000 marines, and 2,000 sailors. The first under Major-General *Ross*—the latter commanded by the famous Admiral *Cockburn*. The troops were a part of *Wellington's* "invincibles." Some works were erecting not far from North Point to arrest their progress; but their incipient state forbade a stand being made at them; and the enemy marched four miles towards us uninterrupted, except by a few flying shots from the cavalry. Here they were met by General *Stricker* with his entire Baltimore brigade, (except that he had only one company of the regiment of artillery) consisting of Col. Biays' cavalry, the rifle corps, and the 5th, 6th, 27th, 39th and 51st regiments of infantry, commanded respectively by Lieut. Cols. *Sterett*, *M'Donald*, *Long*, *Fowler* and *Amey*. In the 5th was incorporated an elegant uniformed company of volunteers from *York*, Penn., under Capt. *Spangler;* and in the 39th, Captain *Metzger's* fine company of volunteers from *Hanover*, Penn., and Capt. *Quantril's* from *Hagerstown*, Maryland; and in the 6th, Capt. *Dixon's* volunteers from *Marietta*, Penn.—all the rest were city troops; and the whole, including Capt. *Montgomery's* company of artillery (with 6 four pounders) amounted to about 3,200 men. The rest of our forces were judiciously stationed in or near the various defences, &c. About 1 o'clock a party of 150 or 200 men, consisting of Capt. *Levering's* and Capt. *Howard's* companies of the 5th regiment, and Capt. *Aisquith's* rifle corps, were detached from the line to feel the enemy, and bring on the battle; they were accompanied by a few artillerists with one of their pieces. Before they expected it, they were attacked by the British, in very superior numbers, and driven in with some loss after a few fires, to the main body. As the enemy advanced, the artillery opened a destructive fire upon them, which was returned from 2 nine pounders, and the action became general along the line of the 5th and 27th, which were in front. The 39th and 51st were in the rear of these, and the 6th advantageously posted still nearer the city, to protect and cover the whole. The fire from the two first named regiments, as well as from the artillery,* was very active and uncommonly certain for about an hour. Of the 5th, much was expected, but the 27th behaved, at least as gallantly. The men took deliberate aim, and the carnage was great—the "*invincibles*" dodging to the ground, and crawling in a bending posture, to avoid the militia—the "yeomen" they were taught so much to despise. When the 5th and 27th (between which was placed the artillery) were outflanked by the much greater f rce of the enemy, they retired in better order than could have been expected under a galling fire; and they retired reluctantly at the repeated command of their officers. The artillery had been drawn off a little while before. The right of the 39th was gallantly engaged, but the 51st took no part in the action; and it was not at that time and place expected that the 6th would share in it, else (under its veteran Colonel, a soldier of the revolution, and one who met the same foe under *Pulaski*) it would, no doubt, have distinguished itself. The cavalry, though they performed very severe and important duties, had but little to do in the battle. The whole number of our men actually engaged did not exceed 1,700.

Nearly as much, perhaps, being done at this point as was expected, our force retreated towards the city. The enemy followed slowly, and on Tuesday night approached within about two miles of our entrenchments. Measures were taken to cut them off and punish their temerity; but before General *Winder* with the Virginia militia, and a squadron of the United States cavalry, could bring his plans fully to bear, the British suspecting the design or not liking the appearance of our works, decamped suddenly in the night and embarked with such precipitation that, though closely pursued, a few prisoners only were taken. But the pursuing force merited and have received the thanks of their general; and the whole body collected is entitled to the gratitude of *Baltimore* and of their coun'ry, for the sufferings they so patiently and patriotically endured, being compelled to sleep, if sleep was allowed, in the open air, with the heavens for their canopy, for four nights, during the chief part of which it rained pretty constantly and sometimes heavily. They also received their refreshments irregularly; the whole being packed up in prudent preparation of events that *might* have happened.

But the attack on fort *M'Henry* was terribly grand and magnificent. The enemy's vessels formed a great halfcircle in front of the works on the 12th, but out of reach of our guns, and also those of the battery at the *Lazaretto*, on the opposite side of the great cove or basin around the head of which the city is built. Fort M'Henry is about 2 miles from the city, a "light little" with some finely planned batteries, mounted with heavy cannon, *as the British very well know*. At 6 o'clock on Tuesday morning, six bomb and some rocket vessels commenced the attack, keeping such a respectful distance as to make the fort

---
*The artillery fired about 130 rounds.

rather a *target* than an opponent; though Major *Armistead*, the gallant commander, and his brave garrison fired occasionally to let the enemy know the place was not given up!! Four or five bombs were frequently in the air at a time, and, making a double explosion, with the noise of the *foolish* rockets and the firings of the fort, Lazaretto and our barges, created a horrible clatter. [Many of these bombs have since been found entire—they weigh, when full of their combustibles, about 210 or 220 lbs., and they threw them much further than our long 42 pounders would reach.] Thus it lasted until about 3 o'clock in the afternoon, when the enemy, growing more courageous, dropped nearer the fort, and gave the garrison and batteries a little of the chance they wanted. The balls now flew like hail-stones, and the Britons slipped their cables, hoisted their sails and were off in a moment, but not without damage. When they got out of harm's way they renewed the "*magnanimous*" attack, throwing their bombs with an activity excited by their mortification. So they went on until about 1 o'clock in the morning, our battery now and then firing a single gun. At this time, aided by the darkness of the night and screened by a flame they had kindled, one or two rocket or bomb vessels and many barges, manned with 1,200 chosen men, passed Fort M'Henry and proceeded up the *Patapsco*, to assail the town and fort in the rear, and, perhaps, effect a landing. The weak sighted mortals now thought the great deed was done—they gave three cheers, and began to throw their missive weapons. But, alas! their cheering was quickly turned to groaning, and the cries and screams of their wounded and drowning people soon reached the shore; for Forts *M'Henry* and *Covington* with the *City Battery* and the *Lazaretto* and barges, vomited an *iron flame* upon them, in heated balls, and a storm of heavy bullets flew upon them from the great semi-circle of large guns and gallant hearts. The houses in the city were shaken to their foundations, for never, perhaps from the time of the invention of cannon to the present day, were the same number of pieces fired with so rapid succession; particularly from Fort *Covington*, where a party of *Rodger's* really *invincible* crew were posted. *Barney's* flotilla men, at the *City Battery*, maintained the high reputation they had before earned. The other vessels also began to fire—and the heavens were lighted with flame, and all was a *continued* explosion for about half an hour. Having got this *taste* of what was prepared for them (and it was a mere taste) the enemy precipitately retired with his remaining force, battered and crippled, to his *respectful* distance; the darkness of the night and his ceasing to fire (which was the only guide our people had) preventing annihilation. All was for sometime still—and the silence was awful—but being beyond danger some of his vessels resumed the bombardment, which continued until morning—in all about 24 hours, during which there were thrown not less than 1,500 of these great bombs, besides many rockets and some round shot. They must have suffered excessively in this affair—two of their large barges were found sunk; and in them were yet some dead men. But what the loss really was it is probable we never shall know. They also were at other times injured by Fort M'Henry, the *Lazaretto* and the barges. I myself believe I saw several shot take effect during Tuesday afternoon.

The preservation of our people in the fort is calculated to excite in a wonderful manner our gratitude to that GREAT BEING, without whose knowledge "a sparrow does not fall to the ground." *Only four were killed and about 20 wounded, and 2 or $300 will repair all the damages the fortresses sustained!*

Lieut. *Clagget*, of Captain *Nicholson's* company of artillery, was the only officer killed in the fort. His friend, Sergeant *Clemm*, of the same corps, received his death at the same time. They were respectable merchants.

The Admiral had fully calculated on taking the fort in *two hours*. Its surrender was spoken of as a matter of course. He said that when it was taken and the shipping destroyed, "*he would think about terms for the city!*" All about and in the fort is such ample evidence of his zeal to perform his promise, that it seems impossible to believe that greater damage was not done than was really sustained. The gallant and accomplished *Armistead*, through watching and excessive fatigue (for he had other great duties to do besides defending his post) flagged as soon as the fight was done, and now lies very ill; but not dangerously, we trust, though severely afflicted. Many of his gallant companions were also exhausted, but have generally recruited their strength.

To return to the field engagement. The force of the enemy in the battle may have amounted to 4,000 men. They were fine looking fellows, but seemed very unwilling to meet the "yankee" bullets—their dodging from the cannon and stooping before the musketry has already been noticed. The prisoners and deserters say that for the time the affair lasted, and the men engaged, they never received so destructive a fire: and this may well be, for our men fired not by word of command only, but also at an object Of the 21st British regiment about 500 were landed—on the morning of the 13th they found 171 killed, wounded and missing. Their whole loss may be safely estimated at from 500 to 700 men. Major General ROSS, who did "not care if it rained militia," the *incendiary of the capitol*, paid the forfeit of that act by his death. He was killed in the early part of the action; and there is reason to believe that two or three other officers high in command met the same fate. *Ross* was a brave man and an able commander—and if he had been engaged in *another system* of warfare would have claimed our respectful remembrance. We may admire, but we cannot esteem his memory. The character of *Moor* in *Schiller's* play of the "Robbers," notwithstanding its grandeur, disgusts by the *business* to which his great talents and accomplishments were devoted. So it was with *Ross*. His *orders*, perhaps, may afford some sort of an excuse for his violation of the rules of civilized war. His death was probably the immediate cause why an attack upon our works was not made. General Brooks, on whom the command devolved, would not risk the enterprize.

Our whole loss in the affair was about 20 killed, 90 wounded and 47 prisoners and missing.* The officers killed were James Lowry Donaldson, Esq., adjutant of the brave 27th regiment, and one of the representatives of this city in the house of delegates of Maryland—he fell while encouraging his brethren in arms: and Lieut. *Andre* of the "Gray Yagers," a valuable young man. Major *Moore* of the 27th was severely, but not dangerously wounded. Major *Heath* of the 5th had two horses shot under him, and Major *Barry's* of the same regiment, was also killed. The cavalry lost several horses, and some of them on the look-out were taken prisoners. For the present, we shall only add that Brigadier General *Stricker*, whose urbanity has long endeared him to the citizens under his command, and the people at large, behaved as became the high charge entrusted to him as a soldier. He has the entire confidence of his Brigade. *Robert G. Harper*, Esq.,who volunteered his services as an aid-de-camp, also greatly exerted himself in the hottest part of the fire to encourage and give steadiness to our troops.

The enemy's bomb-vessels, we are told, are much wrecked by their own fire. This may well be supposed when the fact is stated that at every discharge they were forced two feet into the water by the force of it, thus straining every part from stem to stern.

Never was the mortification of an invader more complete than that of our enemy. Beaten by the militia and defeated by the fort, he went away in the worst possible humor, and a total loss that may amount to not less than 800 men.

The following is from a *London* paper of June 17—"It is understood that the grand expedition preparing at Bordeaux for America, under the gallant lord Hill, is destined for the Cheapeake direct. Our little army in Canada, will at the same instant be directed to make a movement in the direction of the *Susquehanna ;* and both armies will therefore, in all probability meet at Washington, Philadelphia or Baltimore. *The seat of the American government*, BUT MORE PARTICULARLY BALTIMORE is to be the immediate object of attack. In the diplomatic circles it is also rumored that our naval and military commanders on the American station have no power to conclude any armistice or suspension of arms. They carry with them certain terms, which will be offered to the American government at the point of the bayonet. The terms of course are not made public; but there is reason to believe that America will be left in a much worse situation,as a naval and commercial power, than she was at the commencement of the war."

---

* Twenty-two of the wounded were paroled on the field—47 are on board the fleet, (many of them gentlemen of the first respectability,) and it is believed will be sent to Halifax, though all possible means to effect their release were used. By a flag they were all liberally supplied.

Copies of letters from Major General Smith of the Maryland militia, to the Secretary of War.

H. QUARTERS, HAMPSTEAD-HILL,
Balt., Sept. 14, 1814—10 A. M.

Sir—I have the honor of informing you, that the enemy, after an unsuccessful attempt both by land and water, on this place, appear to be retiring.

We have a force hanging on their rear—I shall give you further particulars in the course of the day.

I have the honor to be, your obedient servant,
(Signed) S. SMITH, *Major General Commanding.*

P. S. The enemy's vessels in the Patapsco are all under way going down the river. I have good reason to believe that General Ross is mortally wounded.

Honorable James Monroe, acting Secretary of War.

HEAD-QUARTERS, Baltimore, 15th September, 1814.

SIR—I have been so incessantly occupied, that it has been impossible for me to convey to you the information respecting the enemy, which it would have been proper for you to have received from me. A detailed statement will be forwarded as soon as it can be made out; in the mean time, I have the pleasure to inform you that the enemy embarked their rear guard about 1 o'clock, and that their ships, a few excepted, are out of the river; their destination unknown.

I have the honor to be, your obedient servant,
SAMUEL SMITH, *Major General Com'g.*
Colonel James Monroe, Acting Secretary of War.

HEAD-QUARTERS, Baltimore, September 15th, 1814.

SIR—I have the honor to enclose to you, for your disposal, two letters from British officers, received by Dr. McCulloh (garrison surgeon,) whom I had sent to the battle ground to attend our wounded.

I have also the honor to send you enclosed a list of our wounded who were made prisoners, and of the agreement made by Doctor McCulloh respecting them.

I have the honor to be, your most obedient servant.
SAMUEL SMITH, *Major General Com'g.*
Colonel James Monroe, acting Secretary of War.

In consequence of the humanity shewn the following American prisoners of war, I do promise upon honor that they shall not directly or indirectly serve against the British until regularly exchanged.

James H. McCulloh, Henry Brice, George Repert, Jacob Noyle, John Robinson, James N. Marriott, Charles Goddard,

Walter Muskett, Bryan Allen, George Reintzell, Jacob Hubbard, Benjamin Fleetwood, Thomas Brengman, John Pidgeon, Luther A. Norris, David Davis, William Collings, John Lamb, James Davidson, Wm. Keane, jr., James Gibson, Richard K. Cook, Robert Smith, John Jephson, George Bennett, Conrad Euler.

And I do further engage to get the above twenty-six Americans exchanged as soon as possible for a like number of British left at Bladensburg.

JAMES H. McCULLOH, Jr.,
Garrison Surgeon, U. S. Army.

Copy of a letter from Major Gen. Smith to the Secretary of War, dated

HEAD-QUARTERS, Baltimore, September 19, 1814.

SIR—In compliance with the promise contained in my letter of the 15th instant, I have now the honor of stating, that the enemy landed between seven and eight thousand men on Monday, the 12th instant, at North Point, fourteen miles distant from this town. Anticipating this debarkation, General Stricker had been detached on Sunday evening with a portion of his brigade on the North Point road. Major Randal, of the Baltimore county militia, having under his command a light corps of riflemen and musketry taken from General Stansbury's brigade and the Pennsylvania volunteers, was detached to the mouth of Bear creek, with orders to co-operate with General Stricker, and to check any landing which the enemy might attempt in that quarter. On Monday, Brigadier General Stricker took a position at the junction of the two roads leading from this place to North Point, having his right flanked by Bear creek, and his left by a marsh. He here awaited the approach of the enemy, having sent on an advanced corps under the command of Major Heath of the 5th regiment. This advance was met by that of the enemy, and after some skirmishing it returned to the line, the main body of the enemy being at a short distance in rear of their advance. Between two and three o'clock, the enemy's whole force came up and commenced the battle by some discharges of rockets, which were succeeded by the cannon from both sides, and soon after the action became general along the line. General Stricker gallantly maintained his ground against a great superiority of numbers during the space of an hour and twenty minutes, when the regiment on his left (the 51st) giving way, he was under the necessity of retiring to the ground in his rear, where he had stationed one regiment as a reserve. He here formed his brigade; but the enemy not thinking it advisable to pursue, he, in compliance with previous arrangements, fell back and took post on the left of my entrenchments, and half a mile in advance of them. In this affair the citizen soldiers of Baltimore, with the exception of the 51st regiment, have maintained the reputation they so deservedly acquired at Bladensburg, and their brave and skilful leader has confirmed the confidence which we had all so justly placed in him. I take the liberty of referring you to his letter for the more particular mention of the individuals who, new to warfare, have shown the coolness and valor of veterans; and who, by their conduct on this occasion, have given their country and their city an assurance of what may be expected from them when their services are again required. I cannot dismiss the subject without expressing the heartfelt satisfaction I experience in thus bearing testimony to the courage and good conduct of my fellow townsmen. About the time General Stricker had taken the ground just mentioned, he was joined by Brigadier General Winder, who had been stationed on the west side of the city, but was now ordered to march with General Douglas's brigade of Virginia militia and the United States' Dragoons under Captain Bird, and take post on the left of General Stricker. During these movements, the brigades of Generals Stansbury and Foreman, the seamen and marines under Commodore Rodgers, the Pennsylvania volunteers under Colonels Cobean and Findley, the Baltimore artillery under Colonel Harris, and the Marine artillery under Capt. Stiles, manned the trenches and the batteries—all prepared to receive the enemy. We remained in this situation during the night.

On Tuesday the enemy appeared in front of my entrenchments at the distance of two miles, on the Philadelphia road, from whence he had a full view of our position. He manœuvred during the morning towards our left, as if with the intention of making a circuitous march and coming down on the Harford or York roads. Generals Winder and Stricker were ordered to adapt their movements to those of the enemy so as to baffle this supposed intention. They executed this order with great skill and judgment by taking an advantageous position, stretching from my left across the country, when the enemy was likely to approach the quarter he seemed to threaten. This movement induced the enemy to concentrate his forces (between one and two o'clock) in my front, pushing his advance to within a mile of us, driving in our videttes and showing an intention of attacking us that evening. I immediately drew Generals Winder and Stricker nearer to the left of my entrenchments and to the right of the enemy, with the intention of their falling on his right or rear should he attack me; or, if declined it, of attacking him in the morning. To this movement and to the strength of my defences, which the enemy had the fairest opportunity of observing, I am induced to attribute his retreat, which was commenced at half past one o'clock on Wednesday morning. In this he was so favored by the extreme darkness and a continued rain, that we did not discover it until day-light. I consented to General Winder's pursuing with the Virginia brigade and the United States Dragoons; at the same time Major Randal was dispatched with his light corps in pursuit on the enemy's right, whilst the whole of the militia cavalry was put in motion for the same object. All the troops were, however, so worn out with continued watching, and with being under arms during three days and nights, exposed the greater part of the time to very inclement weather, that it was found impracticable to do any thing more than pick up a few stragglers. The enemy commenced his embarkation that evening, and completed it the next day at one o'clock. It would have been impossible, even had our troops been in a condition to act offensively, to have cut off any part of the enemy's rear guard during the embarkation, as the point where it was effected was defended from our approach by a line of defences extending from Back River to Humphrey's creek on the Patapsco, thrown up by ourselves previous to their arrival.

I have now the pleasure of calling your attention to the brave commander of Fort M'Henry, Major Armistead, and to the operations confided to that quarter. The enemy made his approach by water at the same time that his army was advancing on the land, and commenced a discharge of bombs and rockets at the Fort as soon as he got within range of it. The situation of Major Armistead was peculiarly trying—the enemy having taken his position at such a distance as to render offensive operations on the part of the Fort entirely fruitless, whilst their bombs and rockets were every moment falling in and about it—the officers and men being at the same time entirely exposed. The vessels, however, had the temerity to approach somewhat nearer—they were as soon compelled to withdraw. During the night, whilst the enemy on land was retreating, and whilst the bombardment was most severe, two or three rocket vessels and barges succeeded in getting up the Ferry Branch; but they were soon compelled to retire, by the Forts in that quarter, commanded by Lieut. Newcomb, of the navy, and Lieut. Webster, of the flotilla. These Forts also destroyed one of the barges, with all on board.—The barges and battery at the Lazaretto, under the command of Lieut. Rutter of the flotilla, kept up a brisk, and it is believed, a successful fire during the hottest period of the bombardment. Maj. Armistead being seriously ill in consequence of his continued exposure to the weather, has rendered it impossible for him to send in his report. It is not therefore, in my power to do justice to those gallant individuals, who partook with him the danger of a tremendous bombardment, without the ability of retorting, and without that security, which in more regular fortifications is provided for such occasions. The only loss sustained in the Fort is, I understand, about 27 killed and wounded—amongst the former I have to lament the fall of Lieuts Claggett and Clemm, who were both estimable citizens and useful officers.

From General Stricker's brigade, the return of the killed and wounded has not yet come in. It is supposed, however, to amount to about 150—among the former, this city has to regret the loss of its representative in the State Legislature, James Lowry Donaldson, Esq., Adjutant of the 27th regiment. This gentleman will ever be remembered by his constituents for his zeal and talents, and by his corps for his bravery and military knowledge.

I cannot conclude this report without informing you of the great aid I have derived from Commodore Rodgers. He was ever present and ever ready to afford his useful council, and to render his important services. His presence, with that of his gallant officers and seamen, gave confidence to every one.

The enemy's loss in his attempt on Baltimore, amounts, as near as we can ascertain it, to between six or seven hundred killed, wounded and missing—Gen. Ross was certainly killed.

I have the honor to be, with great respect, sir, your obedient servant,

S. SMITH, *Major General Com'g.*

Colonel JAMES MONROE, *Acting Secretary of War.*

Copy of a letter from Brigadier General Stricker, dated

HEAD-QUARTERS 3d Brigade—Baltimore, Sept. 15, 1814.

MAJOR GEN. S. SMITH,

SIR—I have the honor to report to you, that, in obedience to your orders, I marched from Baltimore on Sunday the 11th inst. with part of my brigade, as the advance corps of the army under your command. My force consisted of 550 of the 5th regiment under Lieut. Col. Sterett; 620 of the 6th, under Lieut. Col. M'Donald; 500 of the 27th, under Lieut. Col. Long; 450 of the 39th, under Lieut. Col. Fowler; 700 of the 51st under Lieut. Col. Amey; 150 riflemen under Capt. Dyer; 140 cavalry under Lieut. Col. Biays, and the Union Artillery of 75 men, with six four-pounders, under Capt. Montgomery, making an aggregate of 3185 effective men. I moved towards North Point by the main road, at 8 o'clock P. M. reached the meeting-house near the head of Bear Creek, seven miles from this city. Here the brigade halted, with the exception of the cavalry, who were pushed forward to Gorsuch's farm three miles in advance, and the riflemen who took post near the blacksmith's shop two miles in advance of our encampment. At seven o'clock on the morning of the 12th, I received information from the advanced videttes that the enemy were debarking troops from and under cover of their gun vessels which lay off the bluff of North Point, within the mouth of Patapsco river. I immediately ordered back my baggage under a strong guard, moved forward the 5th and 27 regiments, and my artillery to the head of Longlog-lane (so called) resting the 5th with its right on the head of a branch of Bear Creek, and its left on the main North Point road, while the 27th was posted on the other side of the road in line with the 5th, its left extending towards a branch of Back river. The artillery I posted directly at the head of the lane in the interval between the 5th and 27th. The 39th occupied a ground 300 yards in the rear of the 27th, and the 51st the same distance in rear of the 5th, extending each parallel to the front line. The 6th regiment was thrown back to a position a short distance this side of Cook's tavern, and half a mile in the rear of the second line. My orders were, that the 5th and 27th should receive the enemy, and, if necessary, fall back through the 51st and 39th, and form on the right of the 6th or reserve regiment. The riflemen were ordered to the skirts of a thick low pine wood beyond the blacksmith's shop, with a large sedge field in front, that as the cavalry were still in advance who would inform of the enemy's approach, they might take advantage of the covering of the wood and annoy his advance. I soon learned that the enemy's advance party was moving rapidly up the main road, and as the cavalry continually announced their progress, I flattered myself with the hope that the riflemen would soon proclaim by a galling fire their still nearer approach. Imagine my chagrin when I perceived the whole rifle corps falling back on my main position, having too credulously listened to groundless information that the enemy were landing on Back river to cut them off. My hopes of early annoyance to the enemy being thus frustrated, I threw the riflemen on the right flank of my front line, thereby, with the addition of a few cavalry, very well securing that flank. My videttes soon brought information that the enemy in small force was enjoying himself at Gorsuch's farm. Insulted at the idea of a small marauding party thus daringly provoking chastisement, several of my officers volunteered their corps to dislodge it. Captain Levering's and Howard's companies from the 5th, about 150 in number, under Major Heath of that regiment; Capt. Aisquith's and a few other riflemen, in all about 70; one 4 pounder with 10 men under Lieut. Stiles, and the cavalry, were immediately pushed forward to punish the insolence of the enemy's advance; or, if his main body appeared, to give evidence of my wish for a general engagement. The latter purpose was soon answered; this small volunteer corps had proceeded scarcely half a mile before the main body of the enemy shewed itself, which was immediately attacked. The infantry and riflemen maintained a fire of some minutes, and retired with some loss in killed and wounded; the cavalry and artillery owing to the disadvantageous ground not being able to support them. In this skirmish, Major Heath's horse was killed under him. At half-past 2 o'clock, the enemy commenced throwing rockets across my left flank, which seemed harmless, and had no other effect than to prepare my line for the sound of the artillery, which soon commenced by us on the enemy's right column then pushing across towards my left, and returned by their six pounders and a howitzer upon my left and center. The cannonading was brisk for some minutes, when I ordered my fire to cease until the enemy should get within close range of cannister. Seeing that my left flank was the main object of the enemy, I brought up the 39th into line on the left of the 27th, and detached two pieces of artillery to the left of the 39th; still more securely to protect my left flank. Colonel Amey of the 51st was ordered to form his regiment at right angles with my line, resting his right near the left of the 39th regiment. The order being badly executed created for a moment some confusion in that quarter, but was soon rectified by the efforts of my Aid-de-camp and brigade Majors who corrected the error of Colonel Amey and posted the 51st in its ordered position. The enemy's right column displayed and advanced upon the 39th and 27th. The 51st unmindful of my object to use its fire in protection of my left flank in case an attempt should be made to turn it, totally forgetful of the honor of the brigade, and regardless of its own reputation, delivered one random fire and retreated precipitately, and in such confusion, as to render every effort of mine to rally them ineffective. Some disorder was occasioned in the second battalion of the 39th, by the flight of the 51st, and a few gave way. The fire now became general from left to right; my artillery in the centre poured forth an incessant volley of cannister upon the enemy's left column, who were endeavoring to gain the cover of a small log-house, about 50 yards in front of the 5th; which, however, precaution had been taken to fire, so soon as Captain Sadtler's Yagers from the 5th (who were originally posted therein) should be compelled to leave it. The enemy's line advanced about 10 minutes before 3 o'clock, with a severe fire which was well returned by the artillery, the whole 27th, the 5th except the three companies of Captain Levering, Howard and Sadtler, which were too much exhausted by the advanced skirmish of the two former—and the ordered retreat of the first battalion of the 39th, who maintained its ground in despite of the disgraceful example set by the intended support on the left. The fire was incessant till about 15 minutes before 4 o'clock, when, finding that my line now 1,400 strong, was insufficient to withstand the superior numbers of the enemy, and my left flank being exposed by the desertion of the 51st, I was constrained to order a movement back to the reserve regiment, under Colonel M'Donald, which was well posted to receive the retired line which mostly rallied well On forming with the 6th, the fatigued state of the regiments and corps which had retired, and the probability that my right flank might be turned by a quick movement of the enemy in that direction, induced me, after proper deliberation, to fall back to Worthington's mill; which I was the more persuaded to, by my desire to have the 6th regiment (whose officers and men were eager to share the dangers of their brother soldiers) perfect and in good order to receive the enemy on his near approach to the city. All retired as I could wish, and were ready to act as circumstances might require it. In this situation you found the brigade on the morning of the 13th, somewhat fatigued, but with increased confidence in ourselves, and renewing our preparation for the annoyance of the enemy alone, if deemed proper, or in conjunction with any other force.

I have thought it due to the merits of my brigade, to detail thus fully their whole movement, and I feel a pride in the belief that the stand made on Monday, in no small degree, tended to check the temerity of the foe, daring to invade a country like ours, and designing the destruction of our city. in whose defence some of the best blood of the country has already been spilt, and for whose safety and protection the citizen soldiers of the 3d brigade are ready to suffer every privation, and meet every danger Should report be true, (and I doubt not the fact) that the enemy's commanding officer, *Major General Ross*, was killed in this action, and that the enemy suffered in proportion to his superior numbers I shall feel still more the valuable consequences of our fight.

The conduct of many company officers and privates, was such as I calculated on; that of most of my field officers also merits my particular notice.—Major Richard K. Heath of the 5th, who led on the advance party to bring on the action, behaved as became an officer, the facts of his first horse being killed under him in the first skirmish, his second being badly wounded, and himself receiving a contusion on the head, by a musket ball, in the general action, are ample proofs of his bravery and exposure in discharge of his duty. Lieut. Col. Sterett, and Major Barry of the 5th, gained my highest approbation, and they unite with all in praise of Captain Spangler and his company of volunteers from York, Pa., then attached to their command; also of Adjutant Cheston, who is slightly wounded. Lieut. Col. Long of the 27th, and his field and company officers, did well; this whole regiment were unsurpassed in bravery, resolution and enthusiasm.—My brigade has to bewail the loss of Adjutant *James Lowry Donaldson*, who fell in the hottest of the fight, bravely discharging the duties of his commission. Lieut. Col. Fowler, and Major Steiger of the 39th, did their duty in every respect; they speak highly of the volunteer companies of Capt. Quantril, from Hagerstown, and Capt. Metzgar, from Hanover, Pa. Capt. Quantril is wounded. Captain John Montgomery, commander of my artillery, gained for himself and his company lasting honor. Captain Aisquith, and his company of riflemen, merit my thanks. Ensign Wilmot, commanding the company of United Volunteers of the 5th, and many of his men distinguished themselves. To brigade Majors Calhoun and Frailey, I am under great obligations for the prompt and zealous performance of their duty. To my Aid-de-camp, Major George P. Stevenson, too much praise cannot be given, his industry in every arrangement before the fight, and in animating the whole line, was conspicuous; his zeal and courage are of the most ardent kind, the sprightliness of his manners in the most trying scenes had the happiest effect upon all to whom he had to communicate my orders; and the precision with which he delivered my commands, could be exceeded only by the coolness with which he always saw them executed. He was animated, brave, and useful. Major William B Barney, and Adjutant Lemuel Taylor, of the cavalry, who, having no opportunity of distinction in their regiment owing to the grounds, did me great service, the former in aiding Capt. Montgomery, the latter in conveying my orders through the whole. Mr. Robert Goodloe Harper deserves my thanks. He visited me just before the action; accompanied the advance party, and aided me much throughout. The brave soldiers under my command have suffered many privations, and I recognise among our killed and wounded many valuable men; of which I will make a report in a few days.

I have the honor to be, your obedient servant,

JOHN STRICKER,
Brig. Gen. Com. 3d brigade, M. M.

GENERAL ORDERS.

HEAD-QUARTERS, Baltimore, September 19, 1814.

The enemy having been compelled to retire from before this city, the Major General Commanding takes pleasure in congratulating the troops under his command, upon a relaxation of these severe duties to which they were for some days necessarily exposed. The readiness with which they submitted to privations of every kind was as gratifying to him as the alacrity with which they flew to arms for the protection of the city. He feels a particular pleasure in imparting to every officer and soldier his warm acknowledgments for the zeal they displayed in marching to meet the enemy, whose object by his own declaration is known to be devastation and ruin to every assailable point on the seaboard. It is with peculiar satisfaction the Commanding General seizes this opportunity of acknowledging the very great assistance he has received from the counsel and active exertions of Commodore Rodgers. His exertions and those of his brave officers and seamen, have contributed in a very eminent degree to the safety of the city, and should be remembered with lively emotions of gratitude by every citizen

The successful defence of Fort M'Henry by Major Armistead of the United States Army having under his command (besides his own corps) three companies of Colonel Harris's regiment of artillery commanded by Captains Berry and Nicholson and Lieut. Pennington and a part of the 36th and 38th regiments of United States Infantry commanded by Lieutenant Colonel Steuart, is beyond all praise. Their gallantry and intrepidity enabled them to defend the Fort against every effort of the enemy, and there is no doubt that this intrepid officer will be rewarded by the Government. The voluntary services of

Major Lane of the 14th regiment of United States Infantry were highly useful and duly appreciated by Major Armistead. Lieutenant Newcomb of the Navy, who commanded Fort Covington, and Lieutenant Webster of the flotilla, the city battery, performed their respective duties to the entire satisfaction of the Commanding General.

To Brigadier General Winder he tenders his thanks for his aid, co-operation and prompt pursuit of the enemy. To Brigadier General Douglass with his brigade, and to Colonel Taylor with his regiment of Virginia militia cal'ed into service for the defence of Washington, the Commanding General also makes a tender of his acknowledgments. They have sustained privations with patience, and submitted to a soldier's life with a temper that does them credit. To the officers much praise is due for the discipline they have introduced, for their attention to their men, and prompt obedience to orders.

To Brigadier General Stricker and the 3d brigade of Maryland militia, every praise is due; the city being threatened, it became the duty of the citizens to be foremost in its defence. He claimed the honor, and the brave officers and men under his command hailed with delight the opportunity of meeting the enemy's first attack: he met the enemy and engaged him, and when compelled by superior number to retreat, he effected it in order, and rallied on his reserve, and from thence retired to the ground which had been assigned him near the line. The particulars of the action and the just praise due to each officer, are given by the Brigadier General in his report. He reports the 27th regiment under Colonel Long, as having in a particular manner distinguished itself—he gives due praise to the 5th, under Colonel Sterrett, and 39th under Colonel Fowler. He reports that his reserve under Colonel M'Donald merited his approbation, and that the artillery under Captain Montgomery highly distinguished itself. He applauds in terms which are flattering, the conduct of Major Pinckney's battalion of riflemen, the command of which on this occasion having devolved on Captain Dyer. He mentions in honorable terms the bravery and good conduct of Major Heath of the 5th, who had two horses shot under him, and of Captains Spangler and Metzgar commanding companies from Pennsylvania, and of Captain Quantril with a company from Hagerstown.

The Pennsylvania volunteers without commissions, repaired to the post of danger, chose officers and organized themselves into regiments, performed all the duties of soldiers and have recommended themselves in a particular manner to the attention of the Commanding General. Much praise is also due to Generals Stansbury and Forman. Their men came out principally en masse, and when assembled were to be organized, armed, equipped and disciplined. All this has been effected through their indefatigable exertions. To these gentlemen the Commanding General tenders his sincere thanks. The enthusiasm shown by their men on the approach of the enemy, gave a full assurance that reliance might be placed on them.

The light corps under Major Randall performed in a manner highly honorable the services assigned it, and the Major's conduct evinced a firmness, bravery and talent for a military life.

The excellent discipline and order of the artillery under Colonel Harris, and marine artillery under Captain Stiles, affords a certainty of their good conduct. The regularity that prevails in those corps does them honor and affords an excellent example to others. Fatiguing as were the duties imposed on United States Cavalry under Captain Bird, and the militia cavalry under Lieutenant Colonels Moor, Biays, Street and Tilghman, and Captain Lee, they were performed with an alacrity and promptness highly honorable to the officers and men. To Captain Thompson of the Flying Artillery and his company, the Commanding General tenders his thanks for their unremitting personal attention as his guard, their readiness in carrying orders and the various separate duties assigned them, and to Major Barney and Captain Thompson with their corps of observation for the correct information received from them.

The guns at the Lazaretto were well served by Lieutenant Rutter of the Flotilla, whose conduct in the discharge of that, as well as the highly important duty of advanced night guards to the Fort, has met the entire approbation of the Commanding General. To the committee of vigilance and safety he feels himself under particular obligations to acknowledge the many advantages he derived from their exertions in providing the means necessary for defence.

Such was the determined zeal evinced on the part of every brigade and corps under his command, that the Commanding General is impressed with a full conviction, that had the enemy made his attack it would have terminated in his discomfiture and defeat.

By order of Major General S. Smith,

WM. BATES, *Assist Adj. Gen.* D. M. M.

DIVISION ORDERS.

Division Head Quarters, New-Church Street,

September 15th, 1814.

Brigadier General *Winder* congratulates the troops of his command upon the suspension of the severe duties to which they have been exposed for the last four days.

The Garrison of Fort M'Henry under the command of Major Armistead, are entitled to, and receive, the warmest acknowledgments and praise from the Brigadier General for their steady, firm and intrepid deportment during an almost incessant bombardment for twenty-four hours, during which time they were exposed to an incessant shower of shells.

The militia artillery of the 3d brigade under Captains Nicholson and Berry, and Lieutenant Pennington, vied with the regulars in a firmness and composure which would have honored veterans, and prove that they were worthy to co-operate with the regular artillery, infantry and sea fencibles in defence of that important post. Major Armistead receives also the warmest acknowledgments of the Brigadier General Commanding for his able, vigilant and exact arrangements before and during this period of arduous duty, as well as for the uniform zeal, vigor and ability he has discovered in his preparations for the defence of the post immediately committed to his charge, as for the prompt and efficacious manner in which he has complied under great and perplexing difficulties with demands from all quarters for ammunition.

Lieutenant Colonel Steuart and Major Lane, neither of whom were required to expose themselves in this dangerous post, will please accept the Brigadier General's warmest acknowledgments for the handsome and gallant manner in which they volunteered to take command of the regular infantry; who with their officers and men, have evinced the most resolute and steady intrepidity in the midst of imminent and long continued danger.

The squadron of the United States Light Dragoons under Captain Bird, have proved by the indefatigable and bold manner in which they have constantly kept upon the very lines of the enemy under the fire of his guards and the regular, and exact intelligence which they have constantly given of his situation, that they want nothing but an opportunity to signalize themselves. The bold and intrepid charge which Sergeant Keller, of Captain Bird's company, made upon the rear guard of the retreating enemy with but three dragoons in which he dispersed a guard of 18 fusileers, taking six of them prisoners in despite of their fire and that of a four pounder within half cannister distance which made three discharges at him, deserves the highest approbation, and the skill and dexterity with which he accomplished this bold achievement proves he will be competent to a more considerable command to which the justice of his Government will no doubt advance him.

Brigadier General Douglass with his entire brigade of Virginia militia have evinced during four days of the most active and arduous duties, under the severest privations of rest and refreshment, in constant exposure to the unusual inclemency of the weather for the season, a patience, obedience, and alacrity for the most dangerous duties which cannot be surpassed; and the prompt and eager pursuit in which they yesterday engaged, after the retreating enemy, in the midst of heavy and constant rain after such a series of suffering and fatigue, is the best evidence which can be given that the patriotism which so promptly led them to the field in defence of their country, was bottomed upon a courage which danger and difficulty cannot subdue.

Lieutenant Col. Griffin Taylor with his regiment also of Virginia militia who was left in charge of the defences in part on the Ferry-branch, has proved by his judicious arrangements and the zealous manner in which he was supported by his men and officers, that he only wanted an occasion to prove himself and them the worthy coadjutors of their countrymen.

The enemy has retired from our city and it is to be hoped under such circumstances as will deter him from again attempting it. Those gallant Virginians will have the consolation of believing they have essentially contributed to its safety.

The enemy however has at present only taken refuge in his ships—he still remains in our vicinity and may and probably will return if he knows there is the least relaxation of vigilance or readiness. The Commanding officers of corps and detachments will therefore exert themselves with unremitted diligence to repair the damages of the late fatigue and exposure—to refresh their troops and hold them in readiness for moving at a moment's warning.

By order.   ROBT. G. HITE,
Assistant Adjutant General.

DISCHARGE OF THE BALTIMORE MILITIA.

Adjutant General's Office, 10th *Military District.*

Baltimore, 18th Nov., 1814.

GENERAL ORDERS. The whole of the 3d Maryland brigade, with the exception of Capt. Thompson's troop, Lieutenant Colonel Harris's regiment artillery and Captain Stiles' corps of marine artillery, will as soon as mustered to-day, consider themselves discharged from the service of the United States.

The Major General in taking leave of this fine body of citizen soldiers, who have done themselves and country so much honor, offers to them the thanks of the United States, for their distinguished services.

To Lieutenant Colonel McDonald, who has for a short time commanded the brigade, the Major General tender his thanks, personally, for his prompt and strict attention to duty; also to Lieutenant Colonel Sterrett, whose attentions to the guard for head quarters, furnished from his handsome regiment, have been highly pleasing.

The regiments and corps discharged will turn over to the military store keeper, the arms, ammunition, accoutrements and knapsacks, which have been received from the United States. The arms received from the State of Maryland will be retained by the troops.

(Signed)   W. SCOTT.
By command,   FRANCIS S. BELTON,
Assistant Adjutant General.

List of the killed and wounded of the third brigade, at the late engagement at Long Log Lane, September 12, 1814.—— Communicated to the editor of the Register by Major Frailey.

Captain Montgomery's Artillery.

Wounded—Jos. R. Brookes, 2d Lieutenant, 1 Sergeant and 12 privates, one since dead.

5th regiment infantry.

Killed—6 privates.
Wounded—Captain Stewart, Lieutenant Reese, 1 Sergeant, 2 Corporals and 40 privates.

27th regiment infantry.

Killed—Adjutant Jas. L. Donaldson and 8 privates.
Wounded—Major Moore, 2 Sergeants, 2 Corporals and 41 privates.

39th regiment infantry.

Killed—8 privates.
Wounded—Captain Quantril, 2 Corporals and 20 privates.

51st regiment infantry.

Killed—8 privates.
Wounded—Ensign Kirby and 3 privates.

Rifle battalion.

Killed—Lieutenant Andre and 2 privates.
Wounded—2 Sergeants and 5 privates.

RECAPITULATION.

Killed—1 Adjutant, 1 subaltern and 22 privates.
Wounded—1 Major, 2 Captains, 3 subalterns, 12 non. com. officers and privates.——Total 213.

The recapitulation contains the aggregate of prisoners taken by the enemy, excepting those paroled at the meeting house, included in the wounded. I am unable at present to state to what regiment they were attached. As the honorable Colonel Brook has vied with his companions in falsifying an *official* report, I beg you will favor the public with this account in any form you please. I pledge myself for its correctness.

Yours respectfully,

L. FRAILEY, late Brig. Maj.
3d Brigade M. M.

1814-1889.

MARYLAND EXPOSITION.

"GUARD OF HONOR."

MORRIS PUTNAM STEVENS,
　　　　　　　　Chief Marshal,

SEPTEMBER 9TH, 1889.

DESCENDANTS OF BALTIMORE'S DEFENDERS.

Battle at North Point, 1814.

MORRIS PUTNAM STEVENS, 1320 Linden ave.
Great grandfather, Captain Jehu Bouldin, of "The Independent Light Dragoons, 5th Regiment Maryland Cavalry, militia, Lieut. Col. James Biays, Third Brigade, Brigadier General John Stricker.

CAPT. JOSEPH H. J. RUTTER, 205 S. Chester St., is the son of Lieutenant Solomon Rutter, United States Navy, under Commodore Barney in Barney's flotilla. The sons of Capt. Joseph H. J. Rutter, grandsons of Lieut. Solomon Rutter, are Joseph W. Rutter, Charles E. Rutter, Frank Solomon Rutter, and Harry Gill Rutter (youngest 17 years old).

Commodore Rogers, in his report of the bombardment of Fort McHenry, refers to Lieut. Solomon Rutter, commending him for sending Capt. Webster to place obstructions in the harbor, to prevent the British ships from coming up to the city.

DR. H. STARR.
Father, William Starr; uncle, Hezekiah Starr, privates American Artillerists, Capt. R. B. Magruder.

JEFFERSON RAMSAY, 912 Harlem ave.
Father, John Ramsay, private in 6th Regiment, under Capt. Robt. Conway.

WM. L. BUCK, 623 Patterson Park ave.
Grandfather, John Buck, Trumpeter of Independent Light Dragoons. Grandfather, Phillip Shillang.

SAML. A. DOWNS, 407 Warren st.
Grandfather, Thos. Neving, Fell's Point Riflemen. Has rifle, bullets, &c.

ROBERT T. SMITH, 102 Fayette st.
Father, Benjamin B. Smith, private Marine Corps, Captain George Stiles, commanding.

GEORGE H. BOULDIN, 949 N. Washington st.
DALRYMPLE BOULDIN, Hoffman st., near Gay.
Brothers. Sons of Henry Bouldin, and grandsons of Capt. Jehu Bouldin, Independent Light Dragoons.

GEO. F. BOULDIN, son of George H.
ALFRED BOULDIN, son of Dalrymple Bouldin.
HARRY THOMPSON, 1814 Biddle st.
Son of Elizabeth Bouldin, daughter of Henry Bouldin.

WILLIAM THOMPSON.
Son of Elizabeth Bouldin, daughter of Henry Bouldin.
WM. WEINKENICHT, 1316 Holland st.
Son of Mary Bouldin, daughter of Henry Bouldin.
FRANK MEDCALFE, 1618 Riggs ave.
Father, William M. Medcalfe, private under Capt. Peter Pinney, 27th Regiment, Lieut. Col. Kennedy Long, commanding.
JOSEPH H. HELM, 339 N. Stricker st.
Father, Leonard Helen, private in Washington Artillery Co., Capt. Berry. J. H. H. has his sword and scabbard.
WILLIAM OWINGS SOLLERS, E. Baltimore st., cor. Dallas.
Grandfather, Fred. Seyler, private in Capt. Sterrett's Company, 5th Reg. of Infantry, Lieut. Col. Joseph Sterrett, commanding.
FRANK W. CASSARD 205 N. Howard st.
Sons, Samuel S., Gilbert, and Douglas. Father, Gilbert Cassard, private in Washington Artillery, Capt. John Berry, 5th Regiment.
J. BROWN BAXLEY, S.E. cor. Madison ave. and McMechin st
Father, George Baxley, private Washington Artillery, Capt. John Berry. Has a shell taken from field by his father; weight 195 pounds.
DR. J. BROWN BAXLEY, Jr.
Grandfather, George Baxley.
HENRY M. BAXLEY. Same.
WM. HENRY BAXLEY, Tinner, Lombard st.
Father, Jos. M. Baxley, at North Point.
HAUGHTON BAXLEY, 102 E. Franklin st.
Great grandfather, George Baxley. See above.
ROBERT P. BROWN, 1408 Linden ave. Now Captain in the 5th Regiment, M. N. G.
Grandfather, Patrick Caughy, private in Capt. Michael Haubert's Company, 51st Regiment Maryland militia. Henry Amey, Lieut. Colonel commanding.
GEORGE HENRY STICKNEY, of Reed, Stickney & Co.
Grandfather, Henry Stickney, private in Baltimore Fencibles, Capt. Nicholson
HENRY S. and GEORGE LEWIS STICKNEY.
Sons of Geo. Henry Stickney, but too young to participate. G. H. S. has a number of relics.
A. J. EVANS and BROTHER, 1419 E. Preston st.
Grandfather, Thomas Evans, at North Point; a member of Old Defenders' Association; private under Capt. Thomas L. Lawrence, 6th Regiment, Lieut. Col. McDonald.
JAS. D. STANSBURY, 134 S. Broadway.
Grandfather, Dr. Jas. B. Stansbury, (see *Niles' Register*, p. 70), Assistant Surgeon in Capt. Thomas Sheppard's Company, 6th Regiment, Lieut. Col. Wm. McDonald.

EDWARD JOHNSON, with Findlay, Roberts & Co.
2223 Oak street.
Grandfather, Edward Johnson, third Mayor of Baltimore. Mayor on Sept. 12, 1814.

FRANCIS E. BOND, 1109 Patterson ave.
J BOSLEY BOND, Tax Department, City Hall
Father, Thos. T. Bond, private in Capt. Chas. Pennington's Baltimore Independent Artillerists.

THOS. T. BOND, Jr., 1031 Fulton ave.
Age 14 years, grandson of Thos. T. Bond.

DR. WM. RUST NEVILLE, Hampden, Woodberry, Md.
Great grandfather, Samuel Rust, private in Capt. Chas. Pennington's Company, "The Baltimore Independent Artillerists," of the 1st Regiment of Artillery of Md. militia, Lieut. Colonel David Harris in command.

BENTON H. WATTS, 202 E. Townsend st.
Father, Thomas B. Watts, private in Capt. Edw. Aisquith's Comp'y of 1st Rifle Battalion, Maj. Wm. Pinkney commanding.

W. H. GRUVER, 1316 N. Washington st.
Father, John Gruver, private Capt. Edw. Aisquith's Company of Sharpshooters, 1st Rifle Battalion, Maj. Wm. Pinkney.

WILLIAM F. LONG, Martinsburg, W. Va.
Father, Jesse Long, private in Capt. George H. Stewart's Company, called "Washington Blues," 5th Reg. Infantry Md. Militia, Lieut. Col. Joseph Sterrett in command.

JOHN W. R. SUMWALT, age 13, 529 S. Charles st.
Great Grandfather, John J. Daneker, private in Capt. Danl. Schwarzauer's Company, 27th Regiment. President Old Defenders' Association.

C. W. BUCKINGHAM, Norfolk, Va.
Father, Levi Buckingham, private Capt. John Shrim's Co., 1st Baltimore Light Infantry, 5th Regiment, Lieut. Col. Joseph Sterrett.

WINTER D. HORTON, 1106 E. Fayette st.
Grandfather, Capt. James Horton, Maryland Chasseurs, 5th Regiment.

RICHARD HENRY LEE, 2006 Maryland ave.
Great grandfather, John Wilson.

ROBERT J. RAMSEY, 1043 Abey st.
Grandfather, Frederick Jordan, private "Baltimore Union Artillerists," Capt. John Montgomery, of 1st Regiment of Artillery, Lieut. Col. David Harris. Father, Robert Ramsey.

CHARLTON G. PENTZ, 203 Aisquith st.
Grandson of Daniel Pentz, private United Maryland Artillery, Capt. James Piper; also, grand-uncle, Henry Pentz, 1st Lieutenant of United Maryland Artillery. Grandfather, John Grosh, private "Eagle Artillerists," Capt. George J. Brown (John Grosh, 1st cousin of Francis Scott Key. Their mothers name was "Charlton").

SAML. C. AND CHAS. K. CANNON, brothers, 203 Aisquith st.
Great grandfather, Daniel Pentz.

WM. WRIGHT BECK, age 14, 203 Aisquith st.
Great grandfather, Daniel Pentz.

FRANCIS ASBURY MILLER, 1815 Eager st.
Father, Andrew Miller, private in Capt. Jacob Deems Co., of 51st Regiment, Lieut. Col. Amey.

LEWIS H. MILLER, 1815 Eager st.
Grandson of Andrew Miller.

RICHARD F. MILLER, age 15.
Great grandson of Andrew Miller.

SAMUEL RICHARDSON.
Great great-grandson of Andrew Miller.

SAML. F. PRIMROSE, Circuit Court.
Grandfather, Joseph Hush, private in Capt. McGee's Comp'y.

WM. MALCOLM SEATON, SAML. F., JR., and HARRY P. PRIMROSE, (sons of S. F.)
Great grandfather, Joseph Hush, killed at Loudenslager's Hill.

GEO. W. SEWELL, Avalon, Baltimore co., Md.
Father, Josiah Sewell, private in Capt. John De Bell's Comp'y in a Virginia Regiment, under Col. McMullin. G. W. S. member Old Defenders' Association.

G. H. FULTON, Church Home and Infirmary, Broadway.
Grandfather, Lieut. Colonel David Harris, commanding 1st Regiment of Artillery.

J. MORRISON HARRIS.
Father, Col. David Harris.

WM. HALL HARRIS.
Grandfather, Col. David Harris.

CHAS. H. RAY, 1516 E. Preston st.
Grandfather, Benj. Germain, 3d Sergt. of "United Maryland Artillery," Capt. James Piper, of the 1st Regt. of Artillery.

J. WILSON RAY, 13 years, 1516 E. Preston st.
Great grandfather, Benjamin Germain.

BENJ. C. GERMAIN, care of Turner Bamberger, cor. Madison and Chew streets.
Father, Benj. Germain.

JOHN EDWIN WARNER, 1303 Division st.
Grandson of Mrs. Elizabeth Sands. Capt. Andrew Ellicott Warner, grandfather of J. E. Warner, Captain of a Company in 39th Regiment. John Warner, grand uncle of J. E. W., and brother of Capt. Warner (above), private in Capt. Edw. Aisquith's Company of Sharpshooters, 1st Rifle Battalion, Wm. Pinkney, Major commanding.

GEO. C. WARNER, Etting st., near Dolphin.
Grandfather, Capt. Andrew E Warner, etc.

T. S. WATERS, JR., cor. Lafayette and Arlington aves.

Great grandfather, Jacob Grafflin. Ignatius Waters at Bladensburg.

JOHN H. ROGERS, 1329 N. Carey st.

Father, John H. Rogers, Captain in 51st Regiment. Has sword and epaulettes.

Sons of John H. Rogers
- JOHN H. ROGERS, Jr., Philadelphia, Pa.
- MICHAEL W. ROGERS, U.S. Ex. Officer, Barre st.
- FRANK L. ROGERS, Kingston, N. Y.
- GEORGE R. ROGERS, Hotel Rennert.
- CHAS. A. ROGERS, 1329 N. Carey street.

FREDERICK W. SCHMINKE, 649 German st.

Father, Geo. Schminke, private in Capt. Sadtler's Company Baltimore Yeagers, 5th Regiment Infantry, Md. militia, Lieut. Col. Joseph Sterrett. Has cert. of mem. of his father in Old Defenders' Association, 1842.

WM. C. SCHMINKE, Ohio.

JOHN H. MILLER, N. E. cor. Baltimore and Calhoun sts.

Father, Christopher Miller, private in Capt. Horton's Company Maryland Chasseurs, 5th Regiment Md. Cavalry, Lieut. Col. Jas. Biays.

JOSEPH A. GILPIN, 1309 Linden ave.

Great grandfather, Jesse Levering, private in Capt. Samuel Sterrett's Company, (Independent Company), 5th Reg. Infantry, Maryland Militia, Lieut. Col. Sterrett, commanding.

WALTER B. MAYNARD, EGBERT P. MAYNARD, brothers, 1425 Aliceanna st.

Great grandfather, Capt. Foster Maynard.

J. OWEN DORSEY, Takoma Park P. O., D. C., box 78.

Grandfather, James Hance, private in the "Independent Blues," Capt. Aaron Levering, of 5th Regiment of Infantry of Maryland Militia, Lieut. Col. Joseph Sterrett, commanding.

R. LEE GILL, 110 St. Paul st.

Great grandfather, Capt. Stephen Gill.

GEORGE CORBIN ROSE, 912 Calhoun st.

Father, Jacob Andrew Rose, (J. Roesener in Hickman), private in Capt. Philip B. Sadtler's Co., Baltimore Yeagers, 5th Regiment of Infantry, Joseph Sterrett, Lieutenant Colonel, in command.

BENJAMIN BREVARD NICOLL, 714 N. Fulton ave.

Father, Thomas Nicoll, private Fell's Point Riflemen, Capt. Wm. B. Dyer, Major Pinkney, 1st Rifle Battalion.

THOMAS YOUNG NICOLL, and BENJAMIN BREVARD NICOLL, Jr, 13 years, sons of B. B. N., 714 N. Fulton ave.

SAMUEL LEVI COLLMUS, 406 N. High st.

Grandfather, Levi Collmus, private, United Maryland Artillery, Capt. James Piper.

GEO. C. DANEKER, 1243 W. Lombard st.

Father, John J. Daneker, private in Capt Daniel Schwarzauer's Company, 27th Regiment, Md. militia.

HARRY A. L., WILLIE and CHARLES GRUBB, brothers, 1516 E. Preston st , with Chas. H. Ray.

Great grandfather, Benjamin German, 3d Sergt. of United Md. Artillery, Capt. James Piper, 1st Regiment.

JOHN T. DEALE (son), 1424 N Bond st., and JOHN T., Jr., EDWD. B., WM. J., ROBT. S. and WALTER DEALE, 1424 N. Bond st.

Great grandsons of Thos. Stewart, private Capt. John Montgomery's Company "Baltimore Union Artillery," 1st Regiment Artillery, Md. militia, Lieut.Col. David Harris, 3d Brigade.

DAVID LACY McGLENAN, 237 Falls Road, Hampden

Grandfather, Jesse James, 2d Sergt United Maryland Artillery, Capt James Piper, 1st Regiment of Artillery, Md. militia, Lieut. Col. David Harris.

EDW. F. ALLEN, Cashier Empire Line, corner Centre and Davis streets.

Great grandson of Jesse James.

E. SMITH DICKEY, 2129 N. Charles st.

Grandfather, Capt. Philip B. Sadtler, of the "Baltimore Yeagers," 5th Regiment Infantry, Md. militia, Lieut. Col. Joseph Sterrett. See past descendants of Capt. Sadtler.

DANIEL SHANE, 1418 W. Franklin st.

Father, Daniel Shane, private in First Baltimore Light Infantry, Capt. Shrim, 5th Regiment, Col. Jos. Sterrett.

GEORGE, J. RYAN and S. GORDON ARMISTEAD, brothers, South st., near German.

Sons of Christian H. Armistead. Grandfather, Col. George Armistead, commandant at Fort McHenry.

WM. D. WIEGAND, 1011 Madison ave.

DR. WM. E. and HENRY H. WIEGAND, sons of W. D. W.

Father, Daniel Wiegand, private in Capt. Dominic Bader's Company of "Union Yagers," 1st Rifle Battalion, Major Wm. Pinkney.

CHARLES H. MOALE, 1510 Linden ave

Father, Randall H. Moale, "Columbian Artillery," 1st Regiment Md. Artillery, 3d Brigade, Gen. John Stricker.

FRANK B. MOALE.

Grandfather, Randall H. Moale. Has numerous relics.

DR. GEORGE L. HORN, Lafayette ave. and Stricker st.

Grandfather, George L. Reppart, private Captain Schwartzauer's Company, 27th Regiment, Col. Long.

HENRY MOALE, 1922 Madison ave.

Father, Samuel Moale, Captain of Columbian Artillery, 1st Regiment of Artillery, Md. militia.

JOHN, HENRY, Jr., and TRAVERS MOALE, sons of H. M , 1922 Madison ave.

DAVID M. MERRIKEN, 1434 Argyle ave.

Grandfather, Joseph Merriken, private in Captain Thomas Watson's Company, 39th Regiment, Md. militia, Col. Benjamin Fowler. Mortally wounded at battle of North Point. Name on Battle Monument.

CHAS. J. MERRIKEN, 1434 Argyle ave.

Great grandson of Jos. Merriken.

JOS. R. G. WOOD, 232 S. Stricker st.

Great grandson of Jos. Merriken.

WALTER BALL, Agt. Bay Line.

Father, William Ball, private in Capt. John Schrim's Company, "1st Baltimore Light Infantry," 5th Regiment, Lieut. Col. Joseph Sterrett, commanding.

J. EDWIN BALL.

Grandfathers', William Ball and Geo. Schminke.

GEO. HENRY BALL, Light st., near Fort ave.

Son, William Ball.

EDWARD F. CARTER, office *Daily News*, and **GRANVILLE H. CARTER**, brothers, Street's Hotel, Hillen and Forest sts.

Father, Clement Carter.

WM. A. PIET, with Edw. Jenkins & Son.
AMBROSE M. PIET, with Baltimore Publishing Co.
JOHN B. PIET, 304 E. Second st.

Father, John Piet, private in Capt. Levering's Company, "Independent Blues."

JOHN B. PIET, Jr., 416 E. Townsend st.

Grandfather, John Piet.

JOHN PIET, son of J. B. P., Jr.

Great grandfather, John Piet.

CLIFFORD TAYLOR, 627 Saratoga st.

Grandfather, William Taylor, private, Capt. John McKane's Co., 27th Regiment.

MATTHEW TAYLOR, Mount Winans, Baltimore Co.

Father, William Taylor.

WM. T. HENNING, 332 Presstman st.

Great grandson, William Taylor.

SAMUEL A DOWNS, 407 Warren ave.

Grandfather, Thomas Neven, private, Capt. Saml. McDonald's Co., 6th Regiment. Has solid shot, Ft. Covington.

JAMES M DEEMS, 801 Hollins st.

Father, Jacob Deems, Captain in 51st Regiment, Col. Henry Amey.

J. HARRY DEEMS, 910 Arlington ave.
CHARLES W. DEEMS, Central City, Col.
Lt. CLARENCE DEEMS, 4th Art., U.S.A., St. Augustine, Fla.

DESCENDANTS OF CAPT. PHILIP B. SADTLER.

SONS.

CHRISTOPHER COLUMBUS SADTLER, 217 Huntingdon ave.
PHILIP BENJ. SADTLER, 14 Huntingdon ave.

GRANDSONS.

Sons of William, deceased.

PHILIP BENJ. SADTLER, Huntingdon ave., near Barclay street
WM. J. SADTLER, " " "
WALTER SADTLER, " " "
MORGAN D. SADTLER, " " "

Sons of G. W., deceased.

CHAS. HERBERT SADTLER, Baltimore Circuit Court.
GEO. W. SADTLER, Baltimore st., near Charles.
FRANK R. SADTLER, " " "
ERNEST SADTLER, " " "

Sons of Rev. Philip Benj. Sadtler.

SAML. P. SADTLER, Philadelphia, Pa.
REV. WM. SADTLER, " "
PHILIP BENJ. SADTLER, JR., 14 Huntingdon ave.
EDWIN S. SADTLER, " "
JOHN P. SADTLER, " "
ALBERT SADTLER, " "

Sons of C. Columbus Sadtler.

J. P. BENJAMIN SADTLER, 14 Huntingdon ave.
C. C. SADTLER, JR., " "

Sons of Catherine E. Sadtler.

EDWIN S. SADTLER, Charles st., near Huntingdon ave.
AUGUSTUS C. SADTLER, " " " "
C. HERMAN SADTLER, " " " "
WM. R. SADTLER, JR. " " " "

Sons of Eliz. J. Sadtler.

PHILIP B. DICKEY, Chicago.
CHARLES H. DICKEY, 2129 N. Charles st.
GEO. S. DICKEY, " " "
EDWIN S. DICKEY, " " "

GENL. GEO. H. STEUART, Carrollton Hotel.
Father, Capt. Geo. H. Steuart, "Washington Blues," 5th Regiment Infantry, Lieut. Col. Sterrett.

JAMES E. STEUART, Carrollton Hotel.
Grandfather, Capt. Geo. H. Steuart.

EDWIN D. CROUCH, 43 E. Montgomery st.

WILLIAM LEWIS, 1618 McHenry st.
Father, Jesse Lewis.

E. STEPHEN LEWIS and C. LEWIS, sons of Wm. L., 1009 W. Mulberry st.
Grandfather, Jesse Lewis.

ALBERT KIMBERLY HADEL, M. D., 209 W. Hoffman st.
Grandfather, Nathaniel Kimberly, private in Capt. Geo. H. Steuart's Company of the 5th Regiment, Lieut. Col. Joseph Sterrett.

GEORGE STILES, (15 yrs.) and DOUGHLASS STILES, (13 yrs.), 1114 N. Eutaw st.
Great grandfather, George Stiles, captain " Marine Artillery."

R. VINTON LANSDALE, National Exchange Bank, HERBERT P. and JOSEPH T. LANSDALE.
Grandfather, Joseph Tucker, private in Capt. Benj. Ringgold's Company, 6th Regiment, Lieut. Col. Wm. McDonald.

THOMAS C. RUCKLE, with Harry Needham, Pier 18, L'ght st. Wharf.
Father, Thomas Ruckle, 3rd Corporal " Washington Blues," Capt. Geo H. Steuart, 5th Regiment.

THOMAS C. C. RUCKLE, with Harry Needham, Pier 18. Light st. Wharf.
Grandfather, Thomas Ruckle.

WM. THOMAS RUCKLE, Lexington st., near Fremont.
Grandfather, Thomas Ruckle.

WALTER RUCKLE, great grandson, son of Wm. T. R.

T. KELL, AUG. W, and SAML. W. BRADFORD, cor. Lexington and Courtland sts.
Grandfather, Thomas Kell, 1st Lieut. " Independent Light Dragoons," Capt. Jehu Bouldin, 5th Regiment of Cavalry, Lieut. Col. James Biays.

JOSEPH ANDERSON, with Henry McShane & Co.
Great grandson, George Schminke, private "Baltimore Yeagers," Capt. Philip B. Sadtler.

CHARLES L. HALL, Hall Bros. & Co., 36 S. Holliday st.
Grandfather, Capt. John Hall.

PHILIP R UHLER, Librarian Peabody Library.
Grandfather, John Reese, private Capt. Peter Pinney's Company, 27th Regiment, Lieut. Col. Kennedy Long commanding.
Grandfather, Philip Uhler, private Capt. Samuel Sterrett's Independent Company, 5th Regiment Infantry, Md. militia, Lieut. Col. Jos. Sterrett.

JOHN R. KELSO, Jr., Linden ave.
Father, John R Kelso, 4th Corporal Capt. Geo. H. Steuart's Company, " Washington Blues," 5th Reg. Inf., Md. militia, Lieut. Col. Jos Sterrett.

J. RUSSELL KELSO and GEO. R KELSO.
Grandsons of John R. Kelso.

HENRY DUFFY, 207 N. Calvert st.
Grandfather, Henry Duffy, private in Capt. John McKane's Company, 27th Regt, Md. militia, Lieut. Col. Kennedy Long.

WILLIAM ROUSSEY, 1902 Wilkens ave.
Father, Peter Francis Roussey, private in Regular Army at Fort McHenry.

JESSE FEARSON ELY, with Thos. Kensett & Co., 122 West Falls avenue.

WM. H. CARTER, 28 B st. N.E., Washington, D. C.
Grandson of Wm. Heckrote, 1st Sergeant Captain John G. Dixon's Company, 6th Regiment, Lieut. Col. Wm. McDonald.

FRANK STEVENS CARTER.
Great grandson of Wm. Heckrote.

CLEMENT, OSCAR C., CHAS. L., ROBT. D. and HAROLD H. CARTER, 1001 N. Charles st.
Grandsons of Wm. Heckrote. Sons of E. F. Carter.

LESTER F. CARTER, 1001 N. Charles st.
Great grandson of Wm. Heckrote. Son of Harold H. Carter.

GOLDSBOROUGH S. GRIFFITH.
Son of James Griffith.

ISAIAH LaFAYETTE SHAW, 207 Montgomery st.
Son of Isaiah Shaw, late of Captain Benj. C. Howard's Co., Mechanical Volunteers.

CHARLES H. and WM. HENRY SHAW.
Grandsons of Isaiah Shaw.

WILLIAM LAMPING, 1818 Maryland Ave.
Great grandfather, William Starr, private in "American Artillerists," Capt. Rd. B. Magruder.

JAS. B. CLARKE, 406 N. Howard st.
Grandfather, Mordecai Kennedy, private in "Columbian Artillery," Capt. Samuel Moale.

DAVID E. THOMAS, with John M. Carter, St. Paul st.

J. L. SHAW, 144 Montgomery st.

WILLIAM INGLE, Sun Office, Baltimore.
EDWARD INGLE, "   "   "
JULIAN INGLE, Charles County, Md.
Great grandfather, Wm. Pechin. Major of the 6th Regiment Md. militia.

WM. PECHIN INGLE, care of Edw. Ingle, Sun Office.
Grandfather, Major William Pechin.

ROBERT COOPER RASIN, 809 N. Eutaw st.
Grandson of Robt. W. Rasin; also grandson of Jas. Ringgold.

R. W. L. RASIN, 809 N. Eutaw st.

GEO. R. MEDAIRY, J. H. Medairy & Co.; S. B. and J. S. MEDAIRY, 5 N. Howard st.
Great grandfather, Jacob Medairy, 2d Corporal Union Volunteers, under Capt. Christian Adreon, 5th Regiment Infantry, Lieut. Col. Joseph Sterrett commanding, 3d Brigade, Brig. Gen. John Stricker.

CLYDE METZGER KEPNER, 340 N. Charles st.
Grandfather, Capt. Frederick A. Metzger, of Hanover Volunteers, attached to 39th Regiment, Md. militia.

THOMAS L JONES, 1314 N. Stricker st.
Grandfather, Major Thomas S Jones.

THOMAS B. TODD.
ALEX PORTER MORSE, 1505 Penna. ave., Washington, D.C. and DR. EDW. MALCOLM MORSE, brothers, Amossville, Rappahannock co., Va.
Grandfather, Philemon Charles Wederstrandt, an ex-Master Commandant U. S. Navy, volunteered and served under Commodore Perry at North Point.

FRANK WEDERSTRANDT MORSE. son of Dr. E. M. M.
Great grandfather, Philemon Charles Wederstrandt.

MALCOLM EDWARD, CHAS. COLEGATE and FRANCIS M. VAN B. MORSE, St. John P. O., Hernand co., Fla.

BERNARD AUSTIN ROGGE, 831 N. Gilmor st.
Grandfather, Edmund Lewis. Grandfather, Chas. M. Rogge, Capt. P. B. Sadtler's Company of " Yeagers."

JESSE AMBROSE ROGGE, with Nathan Rohr, Baltimore st.

ALBERT NELSON LEWIS, 1811 Walnut st., Philadelphia, Pa.
Father, Elisha Lewis, 3d Sergt. Capt. Pinney's Company, 27th Regiment.

M. CAMPBELL STRYKER, 624 W. Biddle st.
Great grandfather, Roger B. Taney. Great grand nephew, Francis Scott Key.

HEBER HALSEY STRYKER. Same.

ROBERT BENTON DAVIDSON, 2021 Frederick ave.
Grandfather, Henry Lightner, Drummer of " Washington Artillery."

WILLIAM ELLSWORTH DAVIDSON. Same.

ALFRED FLAYHART, 1518 Aisquith st.
WM. H FLAYHART, " "
JOHN J. MAGUIRE, " "
WILLIAM ECCLESTON, Chase's Station, Baltimore co.
ARCHIBALD ECCLESTON, " " "
RICHARD NORRIS McCULLOH, 2408 North Calvert street.
GEORGE WASHINGTON McCULLOH, " "
HENRY LIGHTNER McCULLOH, " "

WILBUR H. RIDDLE, 124 N. Howard st.
Grandfather, Capt. Ishmael Day.

GEORGE H. RODGERS, 831 Edmondson ave.
Father, George Rodgers, private in Capt. Peter Pinney's Company, 27th Regiment.

DESCENDANTS OF NATHANIEL WATTS.

SON.
BENJAMIN WATTS, 1316 North Stricker street.

GRANDSONS.
WALTER W. WATTS, 1316 North Stricker street.
HARRY L. WATTS, " " "

Frank W. Watts, 1316 North Stricker street.
Morris F. Watts, "   "   "

GREAT GRANDSONS.

Benjamin L. Watts, 1316 North Stricker street.
Walter W. Watts, "   "   "
Alpheus W. Madison, "   "   "
Nathaniel W. Taylor, Fowblesburg, Baltimore co., Md.
Walter Taylor, "   "   "
James Howell Taylor, "   "   "
Reuben H. Taylor, "   "   "
Marshall L. Taylor, "   "   "

W. G. MARR, 232 South Stricker st.
R. E. L. MARR, 1500 McHenry st

Great grandfather, Joseph Merriken, private Capt. Watson's Company.

JAMES. W. ALLEN, 2447 Maryland avenue.

Father, Adam T. Allen.

Dr GEO. W. MILTENBERGER.

Father, Gen. Anthony Miltenberger, private Capt. Aaron R. Levering's Co., "Independent Blues," 5th Regiment, Lieu. Col. Joseph Sterrett, 3d Brigade.

GRANDSONS.

WM. BERNARD NEALE, 1531 Bolton st., Baltimore.
ANTHONY MILTENBERGER NEALE.
Dr. LEMOND ERNEST NEALE.
BURNETT NEALE.
HENRY NEALE.

J. THOMAS SCHARF, J. THOMAS SCHARF, Jr., 828 N. Carrollton ave.

Grandfather and great grandfather, respectively, William Scharf, private in Capt. Jacob Deems Company.

WILLIAM F. PENTZ, Jr., 1646 E. Fayette st.

Grandfather, Daniel Pentz, private in Capt. James Piper's Company, "United Maryland Artillery."

JAMES M. COULTER, 1109 Bolton st.

Son of John Park Coulter.

DOUGLAS COULTER, Buffalo, N Y
ROBERT O. COULTER, 1109 Bolton st.
J. MIFFLIN COULTER, "   "   "
WILLIAM M. COULTER, "   "   "
DONALD L COULTER, "   "   "

ROLAND C. WEST, 2129 St. Paul st.

Great grandfather, Gilbert Cassard, private in Capt Wm. Berry's Company, "Washington Artillery."

MARSHALL B. WEST, 2129 St Paul st.

LEONARD J. BANDELL, 2411 York Road.

Father, John Bandell, private Capt. Thos. Sheppard's Company.

JOHN H. BANDELL,   sons of L. J. B., 2411 York Road.
LEONARD J. BANDELL, Jr. "   "   "   "   "
CHAS. A. BANDELL,   "   "   "   "   "
OTIS R. BANDELL,   "   "   "   "   "
GEO. W. BANDELL,   "   "   "   "   "
Has two photographs, battle of Ft. McHenry and North Point

WILLIAM STROBEL THOMAS, 1316 Linden ave.
Great grandfather, John P. Strobel, Corporal "Eagle Artillerists," under Capt. Geo. J. Brown.

JAMES SHELLMAN, Westminster, Md.
Grandfather, Philip Jones, private "Independent Blues," Capt. Levering.

CAPT. JAMES HOOPER, Gay and Lombard sts.
Powder boy on U. S. schooner "Comet," Capt. Boyle, belonging to Commodore Barney's Flotilla.

MORRIS AMES SOPER, 1515 McCulloh st.
Grandfather, Philip Hiss, private Captain George Steever's Company, 27th Regiment, Lieut. Col. Kennedy Long.

WM. WHEELER COLEMAN, 2001 Maryland ave.
Grandfather, Philip Hiss.

WM. H. LIGHTNER, 1518 Aisquith st.
Father, Henry Lightner, Drummer Capt. Berry's Company "Washington Artillery."

CHAS. G. ARNETT, 1712 Barnes st.
Grandfather, Henry Lightner.

JAMES G. ECCLESTON, Chase's Station, Baltimore co.

THOMAS MAGUIRE, 1518 Aisquith st.

JOHN J. WILSON, Marriottsville, Howard co., Md.
Father, James Wilson, Sergeant in Capt. Stewart's Comp'y, 39th Regiment.

Hon. WM. PINKNEY WHYTE, Baltimore.
Father, Joseph Whyte, private Capt. Peter Galt's Company, 6th Regiment. Grandfather, Major Wm. Pinkney, of 1st Rifle Battalion, Stricker's Brigade.

JOSEPH WHYTE, Lexington st.
Grandfather, Jos. Whyte. Great grandfather, Major Wm. Pinkney.

JAMES PENTZ THOMAS, 24 Harford Road.
Grandfather, Sterling Thomas, 4th Corporal, 51st Regiment, Capt James Foster's Company.

PETER B. BROOKS, 1303 W. Cross st.
Father, Wm. Brooks, Eagle Artillerists.

FRANK B. MAYER, Annapolis, Md.
Father, Chas. F. Mayer, private in Baltimore Fencibles, at Fort McHenry, under Gen. Armistead.

CHARLES F. MAYER, President B. & O. R. R., Baltimore.
Father, Lewis Mayer, private in "Baltimore Independent Artillerists," at Fort McHenry, under Gen. Armistead.

JUDGE ROBERT GILMOR, Lexington st.
Father, Wm. Gilmor, private Baltimore United Volunteers, 5th Regiment.

ALBERT and ROBERT GILMOR. Same address.

WILLIAM N. BATCHELOR, 2933 Lancaster st.
Grandfather, William Batchelor, private Capt. Wm. Chambers' Company, 51st Regiment. Lieut. Col. Henry Amey.
Grandfather, ———— Richards.

LITTLETON MORGAN TOUGH, JR., 8 years old, 13 East Lombard street.
Great grandfather, Lieut. Wm. Tough, in Lieut. Col. Francis McClure's Regiment U. S Volunteers (Regulars).

ALFRED LEYBURN PAWLEY, 566 Wilson st.
Grandfather, John Sheldon, private Captain Wm. Chalmers' Company, 51st Regiment, Lieut. Col. Henry Amey, 3d Brigade, Gen. John Stricker.

WM. F. DAVIS, Marriottsville, Howard Co., Md.
Grandfather, Richard Davis.

THOMAS H. WHITE, 104 Commerce st.
Grandfather, John White, private Capt. Aaron Levering's Company.

EDWARD LUCAS WHITE, 104 Commerce st.
Great grandfather, John White.

ENOCH HOLDEN, Farmers' and Planters' Bank.
Grandfather, John Ijams, in war 1814.

E. ST. JULIEN COX, St. Peter, Minn.
Father, William S. COX, with a Pennsylvania Company at North Point.

AUGUSTUS BOULDIN, St. Paul st.
Grandson of Capt. Jehu Bouldin, of Independent Light Dragoons.

OWEN A. BOULDIN, (same).
Great grandson, Capt. Jehu Bouldin.

GEO. W. SEIBERT, 1535 W. Lanvale st.
Grandfather, Geo W. Seibert, gunmaker; grand uncle, John Dunn, also at North Point

GEO. S. STEUART, 326 W. Lexington st.
Grandfather, George Scharar, 1st Sergeant, Capt. William Roney's Company, 39th Regiment.

GENL. RICHARD N. BOWERMAN, 240 Laurens st.
Grandson, Col. James Biays.

DANIEL P. and THOMAS E. WOOD, 248 Clifton st.
Great grandfather, Daniel Wilson, killed at North Point.

REV. BEVERLY W. BOND, Leesburg, Va.
Father, Thos. T. Bond, Baltimore Independent Artillerists, Capt. Pennington.

EDW. A. GAULT, with M. Gault & Sons.
Grandfather, Capt. Peter Gault, 6th Regiment.

WILLIAM THOMAS WAUGH, 1431 E. Monument st.
Grandfather, Jesse Carter, private in Capt. Dillon's Comp'y, 27th Regiment.

EDWD. F. JONES, 17 S. Collington ave.
Grandfather, Jesse Carter. (See above.) Grandfather, John Jones, of Commodore Barney's Flotilla.

JOHN L BARRETT, 223 S. Eden st.
Father, John M. Barrett, under Gen. Armistead, at Fort McHenry.

CHAS. CARROLL and FRANCIS MARION BARRETT.
Grandfather, John M. Barrett (See above) Grandfather, Henry Dorry, Sergeant Fell's Point Dragoons.

REV. JAMES P. SIMPSON, 302 E. Second st., n'r Guilford ave.
THOMAS B SIMPSON.
REZIN B. SIMPSON, JR.
HAMILTON H. SIMPSON.
JACOB S. SIMPSON.
REV. WILLIAM I SIMPSON.
Sons of Rezin B Simpson, private in Capt. Barnes' Comp'y, Maryland militia.

EDWD. WATSON DELCHER, 1338 North ave.
Father, John Delcher, Independent Light Dragoons, Capt. Jehu Bouldin

JAMES H. WOOD, 423 St. Paul st.
Father Nicholas L. Wood, in Capt. Jos. K. Stapleton's Company, 39th Regiment.

JOHN B. MAHOOL, 126 Mosher st.
Great grandson, Lieu. Col. James Biays.

JOHN CASSARD, 2114 St. Paul st.
Father, Gilbert Cassard, private Capt. John Berry's Company, " Washington Artillery."

MAJOR ARTHUR J PRITCHARD, U. S. N.
Grandfather, John I. Stewart, of Commodore Barney's Flotilla.

CHARLES G. KRIEL, 5, 7, 9, 11, 13 Henrietta st , and JOHN F. KRIEL, 5 Henrietta st.
Grandfather, John Kriel, private in Capt. Schwarzauer's Company, 27th Regiment.

CHAS. G. KRIEL, JR., and ANDREW KRIEL.

WM. JAS. DICKINSON HOUGH, 2023 Oak st
Great grandfather, Wm. Stansbury.

GEN. JOHN S. BERRY, Eutaw Place.
Father, Capt. John Berry, " Washington Artillery."

JOHN SUMMERFIED BULL, 1745 Park ave.
B HARRY BULL, 1820 Park ave
R. BERRY BULL, Catonsville.
Grandfather, Capt. John Berry, of the " Washington Artillerists."

J. HENRY HAMLIN, 713 McHenry st.
Grandfather, Henry Peck, private in Capt. Smith's Company.

GEO. P. HAMLIN, (brother J. H. Hamlin).

FRANKLIN PECK, son of Henry Peck, above. Same address.

MICHAEL DIFFENDERFER, 731 Fulton ave.
Father, Michael Diffenderfer, 1st Regiment of Artillery, Col. David Harris.

DR. L. A. MONMONIER, Waverly, Md
Father, F. Monmonier, 2nd Sergt. Fell's Point Riflemen, Capt. Dyer.

STEPHEN BOUIS, JR., 207 N Poppleton st.
Grandfather, Elijah Foreman, private Maryland Chasseurs."

CAPT. JAMES HORTON.

WM. L. RITTER, 541 N. Carrollton ave.
Grandfather, Philip J. Neff, private in Capt. John Findlay's Company, of Chambersburg, Franklin co., Pa.

GEORGE SKAIFE HUGHES, 218 W. Franklin st.
Great grandfather, George Baxley, "Washington Light Artillery."

COL. E. H. WARDWELL, 230 N. Charles st.
Grandfather, James Ackland, 5th Regiment.

WM. M. MARINE, Calvert st., near Lexington.

J. BYRON ALLEN, 2447 Maryland ave.
Grandfather, Adam T. Allen, at Fort McHenry.

JOSEPH F. WILLS, 936 Milton Place.
Grandfather, Jesse James, 2d Sergeant Capt. Piper's Comp'y, "United Maryland Artillery," 1st Regiment Artillery.

WALTER B. WILLS, 1011 N. Arlington ave.
Great grandson Jesse James.

SAMUEL CHASE DE KRAFT, M. D , Cambridge, Md.
Grandfather, Commodore Barney.

MAJOR WM CHASE BARNEY, St. James Hotel.
Father, Major Wm. B. Barney, 5th Regiment Cavalry.
Grandfather, Commodore Barney.

HARRY H. MAHOOL, 126 Mosher st.
Great grandfather, Col. James Biays.

WILLIAM S. DORSEY, 1013 E. Fayette st.
Father, Edward H. Dorsey, private "First Baltimore Hussars," Capt. James Sterrett, Lieut. Col. James Biays.

ROBERT McKEAN BARRY, 1134 Cathedral st.
Great grandson of Col Nicholas Moore, U. S. Regulars, at Fort McHenry.

JOS. ALEXANDER SMITH, 1308 N Holbrook st.
Father, Job J. Smith, Quartermaster under Gen. Stansbury at North Point.

DR. J. H. SCARFF.
Grandfather, Capt. Hy. Scarff, U. S. Regulars, Ft. McHenry.

LANCELOT GAMBRILL and son, Chamber of Commerce.
WM. REUBEN CASSARD, 214 Lennox st.
Grandfather, Gilbert Cassard, "Washington Artillery," Capt. Berry, 1st Regiment Artillery.
FRANCIS F. AHL, 1308 N. Holbrook st.
Great grandfather, Job J. Smith, quartermaster, under Gen. Stansbury, at North Point.
JACOB ALBAUGH, 626 Mosher st.
Father, William Albaugh, Color Sergeant of a Baltimore County Company. (Has the flag carried by his father).
JOHN J. PRICE, 562 Presstman st.
Grandfather, Julius Willard, 2nd Lieu. Capt. Joseph Myers "Franklin Artillery," 1st Regiment Artillery.
FERDINAND and MARION MEARIS, 773 Lexington st.
Father, Jacob Mearis, private Capt. Pinney's Co., 27th Regiment, Col. Long.
COMMODORE FRED. RODGERS and LIEUTENANT JOHN A. RODGERS. U. S. Navy, Washington.
Grandsons of Commodore John Rodgers.
COL. ROBERT J. RODGERS, Snow Hill, near Havre De Grace, Md.
Father, Commodore Jno. Rodgers.
STEPHEN DECATUR McCONKEY, 518 E. Eager st.
Father, James McConkey, Captain in the 27th Regiment, Col. Long.
ROBT. M. CHAMBERS, 1514 John st.
Grandfather, John M. Chambers, private in "Baltimore Union Artillery," Capt. John Montgomery.
HARRY W., C. LEE, HOWARD, CLIFFORD C., JR., JAS. C., CARYL, JULIUS H. and ALAN ROGERS ANDERSON, brothers, 331 N. Carrollton ave.
Great grandsons of Thos. Rogers, private Capt. Nicholson's Company, "Baltimore Fencibles."
HOWARD CLAUDE LIEUTAND, 654 W. Lee st.
Grandfather, John Brown, private "Baltimore Union Artillery," Capt John Montgomery.
MAURICE RIDGELY LIEUTAND.
HENRY B. CHRISTHILF, 1206 Argyle avenue.
AUG. EWALT CHRISTHILF, " "
Great grandfather, John Henry Ewaldt, private in Captain Charles Pennington's "Baltimore Independent Artillerists," 1st Regiment Artillery.
Great grandfather, Henry Christhilf, private Captain Henry Myers' Company, 39th Regiment, Col. Fowler.
GEORGE S. CHRISTHILF, 703 W. Franklin st.
HENRY BASCOM CHRISTHILF, "
Great grandfather, John Henry Ewaldt, private Capt. Chas.

Pennington's "Baltimore Independent Artillerists," 1st Regiment Artillery, Col. Harris.
Great grandfather, Henry Christhilf, private Captain Henry Myers' Company, 39th Regiment, Col. Fowler.

   HENRY T. MARTIN, 1109 McCulloh st.
Father, Samuel B. Martin, Surgeon of 1st Rifle Battalion, Major Pinkney.

   Dr. J. W. C. CUDDY, 506 N. Carrollton ave.
Grandfather, Capt. Lawson Cuddy.

Brothers
- L. O. MERCER, 8 Camden st.
- H. R. MERCER, Calhoun and Pratt sts.
- CYRUS MERCER, Lexington st., near Mount.
- CORNELIUS MERCER, Frederick, Md.

Father, Archibald Mercer.

   SAMUEL M. ARMSTRONG, 1236 E. Monument st.
   J. C. ARMSTRONG,   "   "
Grandfather, J. C. Armstrong, with Commodore Barney's Flotilla.

   HOWARD H. RIDGAWAY, No. 1 N. Calvert st.
Grandfather, John Bennett; great grandfather, Samuel Mills.

   E. J. JOYES, 1008 Cathedral st.
Father, Jesse Joyes.

   JESSE JOYES and I. JEAN JOYES.
Grandsons of Jesse Joyes (above).

EDWARD J. CHRISTHILF. cor. Pennsylvania ave. and
   Green Willow st.
Grandfather, Henry Christhilf, private Capt. Henry Myers Company, 39th Regiment. Grandfather, Henry Dorsey.

   JAMES G. CHRISTHILF, Fremont near Baltimore st.

   LOUIS R. CHRISTHILF, 1714 Druid Hill ave.

   LEROY BROWN, 648 W. Lee st.
Grandfather, John Brown, private Capt. John Montgomery's Company, "Baltimore Union Artillery," 1st Regt. Artillery.

   HENRY BOWERMAN, 112 W. Fourth st.
Grandfather, Col. James Biays.

   LOUIS P. GRIFFITH, 321 St. Paul st.
Grandfather, Howard Griffith, private "Independent Blues," Capt. Levering.

   ROBT. W. McCUBBIN, 33 S. Carey st.
Father, Moses Maccubin, private "Baltimore Fencibles," Capt. Nicholson.

   FRANK BRISCO BRADY, 1513 Winchester st.
Grandfather, David Brady.

ALEXANDER CHAMBERLAIN HOLLIDAY, 1017 N.
   Stricker st.
Great grandfather, Peter Smich.

EDWARD RUTLEDGE PRICE, 40 S. Greene st.
Father, Skelton Richardson, private with Baltimore county troops, Capt. Bosley, Col. Butler.

ROBERT ELLIOTT GERHARDT.
Great grandfather, George Elliott, private "Independent Blues," Capt. Aaron R. Levering.

WERNER SHIPLEY, 913 Fulton ave.
Grandfather, Wm. Hooper. Great grandfather, Benjamin Eggleston, private in Capt. Jacob Deems' Company, 51st Reg't.

WALTER L. RUCKLE, 845 W. Lexington st.
Great grandfather, Thomas Ruckle.

WM. THOMAS RUCKLE. Same address.

JOSEPH and FRANK M. SEWELL, Relay Station, B &O.R.R.
Son and grandson, respectively, of Josiah Sewell.

W. DEALE HALES, 343 S. Gilmor st.
JACOB G. HALES, "   "
Great grandsons of Thomas Stewart, private Capt. Montgomery's Company, "Baltimore Union Artillerists," Col. Harris, 1st Regiment of Artillery.

JAMES T. MITCHELL, 412 E. Pratt st.

THOS. IRELAND ELLIOTT, St. Paul and Fayette st.
Grandfather, John Bunting, private Capt. Michael Peters' Company, 51st Regiment.

WILLIAM G HOLLINGSWORTH, 1419 John st.
Father, Saml. Hollingsworth, Jr., private 1st Baltimore Hussars, Capt. James Sterrett, 5th Regiment, Col. Biays.
Grandfather, Capt. Saml. Moale, "Columbian Artillery."

W. GLENN HOLLINGSWORTH. Same address.
Grandfather, Samuel Hollingsworth.

J. HENRY TSCHUDY, 326 Bloomingdale ave.
Grandfather, Samuel Tschudy.

JOSEPH MERRIKEN CUMMINGS, 118 E. Baltimore st.
Great grandfather, Joseph Merriken, Captain Thomas Watson's Company, 39th Regiment.

CLARENCE H. FORREST, 209 Courtland st.
Great grandfather, Nicholas Snider, ———, Capt Jno. Galt.

C. TAYLOR PENTZ, N. Calvert st.
(Died Sept. 2, 1889.)
Grandfather, Daniel Pentz.

HERBERT WILLIAM RUTHERFORD, 1526 Bolton st.
Great grandfather, Lieut. Wm. Tough, Col. Francis McClure's Regiment U. S. Volunteers (Regulars.)

RICHARD T. FRANCK, 524 N. Paca street.
Grandfather, Henry Wm Gray, private "Baltimore United Volunteers," Capt. David Warfield, 5th Regiment.

CHARLES E. FRANCK. Same address.
Grandfather, Henry W. Gray, &c.

HOWARD LEE FRANCK, 524 N. Paca st.
Great grandfather, Henry W. Gray.

REV. GEO. ARMISTEAD LEAKIN, Lake Roland, Baltimore co., Md., (1900 Park ave.)
Father, Gen. Sheppard C. Leakin, Captain 38th Infantry, at Fort McHenry, under Col. Stewart.

WM. RIDGELY LEAKIN, Savannah, Ga.
J. WILSON LEAKIN, N. Charles st.
Grandfather, Gen. Sheppard C. Leakin.

ST. GEORGE CARL L. SIOUSSAT, Lake Roland.
LENNARD SIOUSSAT, "
Great grandfather.

DR. BENNETT NEALE, 319 W. Monument st.
Grandfather, Gen. Anthony Miltenberger, private in Capt. Aaron Levering's Co., "Independent Blues," 51st Regiment.

JOHN J. WHITEFORD, 310 W. Lombard st.
Father, Samuel Whiteford, from York, Pa.

GEORGE W. WHITEFORD.

W. STRAN McCURLEY, 740 Eastern ave.
Great grandfather, Felix McCurley, private Capt. Andrew Smith's Company, 51st Regiment, Col. Amey. Great grandfather, James McCurley, 39th Regiment, Col. Fowler, private in Capt. Thomas Warner's Co.

WILLIAM J. SHECKELLS, 1741 McCulloh st.
Great grandfather, Adam Smith, private Capt. Peter Galt's Co., 6th Regiment, Col. McDonald.

HENRY HAMMOND, 14 Light st.
Great grandson of Lieu. Col. Jas. Biays.

P. HOLBROOK, 213 Huntingdon ave.
ALF. HOLBROOK, " " "
Grandsons of Frederick A. Crey, of Capt. P. B. Sadtler's Company.

JOHN J. MACDONALD, Waverly.
Grandson of John Macdonald, with a Pennsylvania Co.

FRANK S. EMORY, Hopper, McGaw & Co.
Great grandson of Philip B. Sadtler, Captain "Baltimore Yeagers."

ULYSSES WITZ, 1203 E. Monument st.
Grandfather, Nicholas Elliott.

HERBERT A. SMITH, 933 N. Calvert st.
Great grandfather, John George Bier; Great-great grandfather, John Cunningham.

JOHN H. GIRVIN, (James M. Girvin & Son), Spear's Wharf.
CHAS. Z. BUTLER, 1527 McCulloh st.
NATHAN R. BUTLER.
JOHN W. POWER, 1100 Madison avenue.
WM. POWER OAKFORD, Arlington.
WM. P. ZOLLINGER, JR., 508 E. Lombard st.

JAMES K ZOLLINGER, Louisville, Ky.
HENRY ZOLLINGER, Boston, Mass.
ARCHIBALD CAMPBELL, 1209 McCulloh st.
WM. L. CAMPBELL, 1107 W. Mulberry st.
FRANK CAMPBELL, 1338 N. Stricker st.
THOS. W. CAMPBELL, 1209 McCulloh st.
 Grandsons of Jacob Zollinger, Captain Walker's Company Pennsylvania Volunteers, of Harrisburg, Pa.
 JOHN W. and GEO. E. BROWN, Pratt and Concord sts.
 Grandfather, John Adams Callender, at Fort McHenry, private "Baltimore Independent Artillerists," Capt. Charles Pennington, 1st Regiment Artillery, Col. Harris.
  CHRISTOPHER RABORG, 1314 Lanvale st.
 Grandfather, Christopher Raborg, 1st Sergeant "Independent Company, Capt. Sam'l Sterrett, 5th Regiment.
SAMUEL G. BANDEL, care of F. B. Bandel, "American" office
ANDREW J. BANDEL, "   "   "   "
LITTLETON C. BANDEL. "   "   "   "
FRANK B. BANDEL, "   "   "   "
 Grandsons of Wm. Bandel.
  H. T. MAKIBBIN, 507 N. Fremont avenue.
 Grandfather, Wm. Mops.
  WM. A. BOYD, 1810 Madison ave.
  CHARLES C. BOYD.
  SAMUEL R BOYD.
  WILLIAM A. BOYD, Jr.
  ISAAC DENSON BOYD.
  HARRY B. BOYD.
 Great grandsons of Samuel Rust, private Capt. Pennington's "Independent Artillerists," 1st Regiment Artillery.
  JOHN W. KEPLINGER.
  JOHN B. KEPLINGER, 1630 E. Chase st.
  LEWIS W. KEPLINGER, Petersburg, Va.
 Sons of J. W. K. Grandson of Michael Keplinger, 51st Regiment, in Capt. John H. Rodgers' Company.
  PETER F. SCHLIECKER, Philadelphia, Pa.
 Father, Peter G. Schliecker, under Gen. Stricker at North Point.
  JOHN R DUTTON.
 Father, John Dutton, private in Capt. McDonald's Company, 6th Regiment.
  JAMES B. DUTTON.
 Grandfather, John Dutton. (See above.)
WM. E. B. FAITHFUL, Church Hill, Queen Anne's co., Md.
 Father, Wm. Faithful.
  CHARLES BOBART, 1821 Lexington st.
 Father, C. C. Bobart, Corporal Capt. Thomas L. Lawrence's Company, 6th Regiment, Col. McDonald.

AMBROSE M. EMORY, 1814 Park ave. extended.
Father, Gideon Emory, private "Independent Blues," Capt. Aaron Levering, 5th Regiment, Col. Jos. Sterrett.

AMBROSE M. EMORY, JR. Grandson of above.

AUGUSTINE WALSH EMORY.

SAM'L M. and WM. B. WEAVER, brothers, 908 N. Broadway.
Great grandsons of George Boss, private "Eagle Artillerists," Captain G. J. Brown, 1st Regiment Artillery, Col. Harris.

CAPT. R. NORWOOD, Blue Ridge Summit, Franklin co., Pa.
Father, —— Norwood, at North Point.

HARRY BURTON, 511 N. Howard st.
Grandfather, Jos. Thomas, private "Marine Artillery," Capt. George Stiles.

JOSEPH C. HALL, 403 St. Paul st., near Mulberry.
Father, Jos. Hall, private "Marine Artillery, Capt. George Stiles.

E. A. MILLER, 214 Light st.
Father, Wm. F. Miller, Captain in a Harford County Company.

ANDREW E. WARNER, 303 N. Carey st.
Father, Andrew E. Warner, Captain in 39th Regiment, Col. Fowler.

JOHN THOMAS CARTER, 1128 Fulton ave.
Grandfather, Col. John Carter, at North Point.

CORNELIUS E. B. HAYES, 1276 Battery ave.
Father, John Hayes, private in Capt. Christian Adreon's Co., "Union Volunteers," 5th Regiment, Col. Joseph Sterrett.

JOSEPH PARSONS, 1111 E. Pratt st.
JNO. HY. PARSONS, " "
Grandfather, Joseph Parsons private Capt. Daniel Swarzauer's Company, 27th Regiment, Col. Long.

BYRD G. EICHELBERGER, 34 W. Baltimore st.
Grandfather, Col. Geo. M. Eichelberger.

EDWD. LOUIS REYNOLDS, 1800 Park ave.
Grandfather, John Reynolds.

CHARLES S. LEWIS, 1009 Mulberry st.
Great grandfather, Jesse Lewis.

CAPT. RICH. E. BOULDIN, Belair, Md.
Father, Chas. D. Bouldin.

JOHN T. COOK, 806 Edmondson ave.
Grandfather, Joseph Logan, private, Michael Haubert, Captain 51st Regiment, Col. Amey.

EDW. WM. DORSEY, St. Louis.
WM. LEE DORSEY.
Grandsons of John Reed, volunteer from York, Pa., at North Point.

GEO. BRECKINRIDGE DORSEY.

J. H. R. WARNER, with Keen & Hagerty.
H. W. WARNER.
Grandsons of Michael Warner, at Fort McHenry.

J. SEWELL THOMAS.
Grandson of Sterling Thomas.

CHAS. F. MARROW, 1333 N. Carey st.
Father, Isaac Marrow at North Point.

JAMES W. SHELLMAN, Westminster.
Grandfather, Major Thos. S. Jones.

JOHN L. GRIMES, 936 W. Fayette st.
Grandson of James H. Grimes, at Fort McHenry.

MARION and FERDINAND MEARIS, 773 Lexington st.
Sons of Jacob Mearis, private Capt. Peter Pinney's Comp'y, 27th Regiment, Col. Kennedy Long.

DR. T. CHEW WORTHINGTON, 840 W. Fayette st.
Grandfather, Rezin H. Worthington.

ALEXANDER G. SUTER, 324 N. Gilmor st.
Father, George Suter, at Fort McHenry under Gen. Anthony Miltenberger.

WM. N. CUMMINS, 822 Fulton ave.
Great grandfather, John Keys, 1st Sergeant in "1st Baltimore Artillery," Capt. Abraham Pyke.

Brothers { SUMMERFIELD NORWOOD, 752 W. Saratoga st.
{ CAPT. RANDOLPH NORWOOD
Sons of John Norwood, private Capt. Dobbin's Company, 39th Regiment, Lieut. Col. Fowler.

D. CLINTON SLAGLE, 1227 Linden ave.
Great grandfather, Frederick G. Schaeffer, private "American Artillerists," Capt. Magruder, 1st Regiment of Artillery.

DR. CHAS. C. RICHARDSON, 1622 Edmondson ave.
Father, Dr. Charles Richardson, Surgeon in Fort McHenry.

DR. SAM'L S. RICHARDSON, Colesville, Montgomery co.
MONTAGUE L. RICHARDSON, Washington, D. C.
HENRY W. RICHARDSON, " "
Same as above.

P. HANSON HISS OF WM., 1507 McCulloh st.
Grandfather, Philip Hiss.

REV. A. A. HARRYMAN, Cumberland Valley P. O., Pa.
Grandfather, Stephen Harryman, private Fell's Point Light Dragoons, 5th Regiment, Col. Biays.

SAMUEL S. ADDISON, McMechin st., near John.
Old Defender. Worked in the intrenchments on Loudenslager's Hill.

EDMUND LAW ROGERS, Brig. and Quartermaster Genl.,
Maryland Club.
Son of Lloyd N. Rogers, private Capt. John Eager Howard's Cavalry.

JOSEPH R. WINN, 1429 W. Fayette st.
Father, Christopher Winn, Corporal Capt. Kanes' Co., 27th Regiment.

FRANK RICHARDSON, 330 S. Gilmor st.
Great grandson of Adam Miller.

GEO. W. GILLASPEY, 1035 N. Gilmor st.
ROBT. E. GILLASPEY, " "
Grandsons of John Orem, of Barney's Flotilla.

J. HOWARD SUTTON, 710 E. Biddle st.
Grandson of John A. Callender, private in Capt. Pennington's " Independent Artillery Company."

RIGNALD W. BALDWIN, Jr., 1615 Linden ave.
Great grandfather, Wm. Woodward.

EDWARD B. OWENS, 13 E. Pratt st.

Sons of E. B. O. { **LOUIS CASSARD OWENS,** 13 E. Pratt st.
{ **EDWARD B. OWENS, Jr.** " "
{ **GEORGE C. OWENS,** " "

Great grandfather, Jos. Owens, at North Point, " Independent Company," Capt. Sterrett.
Great grandfather, Benj. Buck, 1st Lieutenant, "Washington Artillery."
Great grandfather, Gilbert Cassard, private " Washington Artillery."

PERCY S. ROSSITER, 822 N. Calvert st.
Grandfather, Jacob Albright, " Lancaster Volunteers."

WM. G. SPEED, 1538 Harlem ave.
Great grandfather, David Davis, private in Washington Artillery, Capt. Berry, 1st Regiment Artillery, Col. Harris.

WM. MASON DULANY, 2416 St. Paul st.
Great grandson of Saml. Dulany, private " Mechanical Volunteers," Capt. Benj. C. Howard, 5th Regiment.

SAML. C. ROBERTS, 2 Elm st.
Father, James B. Roberts, private 27th Regiment.

JOS. O. BARGAR, 1002 S. Sharp st.
Great grandfather, Jos. Bargar, private " Marine Artillery," Capt. Geo. Stiles.

ROBT. T. J. CONWAY, 1505 W. Lanvale st.
Grandfather, Capt. Robert Conway, 6th Regiment.

J. T. GILL, 1203 Argyle avenue.
Grandfather, J. H. Ewaldt.

ALFRED LAPOURAILLE, 1514 Orleans st.
Great grandson of Col. Nicholas Brewer, U. S. Regulars, at North Point.

JOHN A. W. RICHARDSON, 413 Second st., Room 5.
Great grandson of ―― ――, in command of the Six Gun Battery.

GEO D. DUKEHART.
Son of Henry Dukehart, one of the soldiers who carried Wells and McComas from the field at North Point.

JAMES W. ALNUTT.
Son of James Alnutt, private in Capt. Wm. Roney's Company, 39th Regiment.

RICHARD WALTON COOK, Arlington, Md.
Great grandson of Capt. Jacob Grafflin, at North Point.

CLIFTON E. KREBS, cor. Aisquith and Chew streets.
HARRY W. KREBS, " " " "
Great grandsons of Jacob Krebs, who served at Fort McHenry under Commodore Barney.

THOS. L. MATTHEWS, 15 E Fayette street.
Son of Wm. Matthews, private in a Baltimore county regiment.

ANDREW REESE.
Father, John Reese, Lieutenant (afterwards commissioned Captain) in Capt. Samuel Sterrett's Company, 5th Regiment, Maryland militia.

JAMES P. and ERNEST S. REESE.
Grandsons of John Reese.

GEO. D., WM. P. and HENRY O. REESE.
Grandsons of John Reese. See above.

D. J., A. W. and C. P. JUVENAL and DR. J. REESE UHLER.
Grandsons of John Reese.

JAMES CUMMINGS.
Grandson of John Keys, 1st Sergeant Capt. Pyke's Comp'y, "Baltimore Union Volunteer Artillery."

WM. F. DAVIS, Marriottsville, Howard co.
Grandfather, Richard Davis, private Capt. John Woods' Co.

ROBERT LAWSON, 11 E. Lexington st.
Son of Capt. Robert Lawson.

W. NOBLE LAWSON.
Grandson of Capt. Robert Lawson.

JOHN RANDALL MAGRUDER, Annapolis, Md.
Great grandson of Capt. Joseph Hopper Nicholson, of the "Baltimore Fencibles."

FRANK RICHARDSON, 330 S. Gilmor st.
Great grandson of Adam Miller.

JOHN BROWN, JR., 1545 McElderry st.
Son of John Brown, private in Capt. John Montgomery's Company, "Baltimore Union Artillery."

FRANK L. REED, 306 N. Charles st.
Grandson of Robert S. D. Jones, who was a son of James D. Jones, &c.

ROBERT S. D. JONES, 101 N. Exeter st.
Father, James D. Jones, private in 6th Regiment.

JAMES E BYRD, Maryland Steamboat Company.
Grandfather, James Sheldon, private Capt. Chalmer's Co., 51st Regiment.

Great grandsons of James Sheldon. { FLETCHER LEE BYRD. WALTER CUSTIS BYRD. NORVAL EDGAR BYRD.

GEO. NORBURY and HARRY DOWNING MACKENZIE, 22 S. Charlest st.
Grandfather, Thomas Mackenzie, at North Point.

S. HAMILTON CAUGHY.
NOAH WALKER CAUGHY,
MICHAEL P. CAUGHY.
Grandsons of Michael Caughy.

J. H. MAYNADIER, 310 North st.
Grandson of Lieu. Wm. N. Maynadier, of Capt. Mason's Co.

JAMES L. OSBORNE.
Grandson of Capt. Alcorn, Captain of the " Hornet."

E. B GLENN, 135 Elm st., Newark, N. J.,
Old Defender at North Point, private in Capt. Peter Pinney's Co., 27th Regiment.

CHAS. C. CRANE, 1408 McCulloh st.
Grandson of Capt. Aaron R. Levering, of the " Independent Blues."

LEONARD M. FRAILEY.
Grandson of Major Leonard Frailey, also grandson of Sailing Master de la Roche, of the ship " Erie."

GEO. CLINTON McGREEVY.
Great grandson of same.

WM. C. PALMER, 1127 McCulloh st.
Father, Edw. Palmer, private Capt. James Sterretts Co., " First Baltimore Hussars."

THOS. SHEPPARD.
Son of Capt. Thomas Sheppard, 6th Regiment.

THOS. D , SAMUEL McD. and CHARLES SHEPPARD.
Grandsons of Capt. Thomas Sheppard, 6th Regiment.

HUGH BURGESS JONES, cor. Eutaw and Fayette sts.
Son of Ensign Wm. R. Jones, a signal man on Barney's Flotilla.

HUGH BOLTON JONES and FRANCIS COATES JONES.
Grandsons of Wm. R. Jones.

FRANCIS ALEXANDER STEVENS, Kansas City, Mo.
Great grandson of Capt. Jehu Bouldin, of the " Independent Light Dragoons," of the 5th Regiment, Maryland Cavalry militia, Lieut. Col. James Biays, 3d Brigade, Brig. Gen. Stricker.

PROGRAMME
—OF—
CIVIC AND INDUSTRIAL PARADES,
MARYLAND EXPOSITION.

SEPTEMBER 9th-13th, 1889.

THE GREAT CIVIC PARADE.

MONDAY, SEPT. 9th, 1889.

The great Civic and Industrial Parade started from Broadway about ten o'clock A. M., and went over the following route: To Baltimore street, to Eutaw street, to Madison avenue, to Boundary avenue, where part of it continued to Pimlico and part of it disbanded. This was the order of the line:

JACOB FREY, Marshal of Police.
Platoon of Mounted Police.
Maryland colors, United States colors, Baltimore colors.
Trumpeters.
CHIEF MARSHAL, J. FRANK SUPPLEE.
Chief of Staff, Col. CHAS. D. GAITHER.
Mounted Color - Bearer, J. G. BINFORD.
Markers—Capt. GEO. W. CLOTWORTHY and THOS. R. TURNER.

PERSONAL STAFF.

Lieut. Col. Allison Wilmer, C. H. Brace, Thos. F. Putsche, Lieut. Col. George A. Pearre, Louis A. Hazard, Lieut. Col. J. L. Woodford, H. J. Farber, David Whitney, Maj. J. D. Norris, Ed. H. Wise, Col. M. R. Joyce, Alfred Poindexter, Capt. Isidor Becker, A. B. McElroy, Col. F. W. Brune, J. H. Scarff, Lieut. Col. Brent Waters, Wm. S. Wheatfield, Col. J. G. Taylor, Leon Seliger, Major W. O. Bigelow, F. P. Carroll, Captain Noble H. Creager, Robert C. Rasin, J. S. Richardson, Capt. P. L. Perkins, F. Edw. Kingden, Captain H. H. Boswell, N. S. G. Williams, Capt. John W. Cruett, Joseph W. Cochran, Capt. Geo. R. Ash, Frank A. Benson, Capt. Charles G. Wright, Clarence Cochran, Capt. Ed. Roberts, John Parker Haas, Captain C. B. McLean, O L. Rhodes, Captain George R. Browning, M. C. Hodgdon, Percy E. Guard, Capt. W. B. Finney, William McElmoyle, Captain Louis Schneeberger, James Young, C. W. S. Banks, Capt. A. H. Bayly, B. F. Powell, Captain L. S. McNamara, Thomas F. McNulty, Capt. C. L. Dallam, Ed. S. Conlyn, Captain George T. Robinson, George R. McGee, W. C. Rouse, Captain Robert Riddell Brown, Calvin Chesnut, C. J. Taylor, Capt. E. C. Johnson, H. Webster Crowl, Capt. T. H. Shriver, D. Buchanan Merryman, Capt. Henry Mayer, Capt. R. Fuller Shryock, David McClean, R. B. Roache, Capt. D. F. Pennington, A. V. Stevens, Richard Morton, Jr., Capt G. W. Wood, Prof. Adam Itzel, Jr., Lieut. R. M. Lockwood, C. C. Elliott, Emory Barry, Lieut. B. F. Boyden, Armistead M. Webb, Lieut. Thomas Whitridge, W. H. Cox, Joseph Rosenfeld, Lieut. Jas. D. Moulton, Robert S. Wiesenfeld, Lieut. D. M. Hite, W. C. Farber, Lieutenant S. H. Irving, Thomas J. Carroll, Sebastian Brown, S. S. McKim, Thomas R. Clendinen, P. Hanson Hiss of William, Charles M. Roche, Sam. H. Lyon, W. W. McIntire, John Trockenbrot, Dr. H. H. Biedler, Alex. Bechhofer.

GOVERNOR AND MAYOR.

ELIHU E. JACKSON, Governor of Maryland, and FERDINAND C. LATROBE, Mayor of Baltimore.

PRESIDENT FRANK BROWN.

FRANK BROWN, President of the Maryland Agricultural Society, under whose management the Exposition was organized.

THE GUARD OF HONOR.

The Guard of Honor, composed of descendants of men who were prominent in 1812-14. Then came the six divisions, as follows:

FIRST DIVISION.

GEN. GEORGE G. WHEELER, MARSHAL.

The first division was composed entirely of the Posts of the Grand Army of the Republic of Maryland. Gen. George G. Wheeler was marshal, Major Willard Howard was acting assistant adjutant general, and Ira Tyler was chief of staff. The color-bearers were James T. Wesley and Joseph Young. The men who constituted the division were men who, twenty-five years ago, saw service in the war.

Department Commander Wheeler's staff was as follows: John Tyler, Senior Vice Commander; Robt. J. Henry, Junior Vice Commander; George R. Graham, M. D., Medical Director; Rev. Edw. C. Allard, Chaplain; H. A. Maughlin, Assistant Adjutant General; John W. Worth, Assistant Quartermaster General; Alfred S. Cooper, Inspector; J. C. Mullikin Judge Advocate; A. G. Alford, Chief Mustering Officer.

Past Department Commanders.—Graham Dukehart, George W. F. Vernon, Theo. F. Lang.

Council of Administration.—William F. Knight, Samuel F. Pray, I. D. Oliver, Richard J. James, Robert H. Cameron.

National Aides-de-Camp.—H. A. Barry, Edward Schilling, John Bowers, John R. Bailey, John R. King, Thomas H. Coburn, Dallas Langley, J. B. McClure, John W. McCullough, A. H. Hyson, John W. Kaufman, William T. Robinson.

Aides-de-Camp.—N. M. Rittenhouse, Daniel T. Senton, Geo. W. Grove, Henry Ewalt, Wm Lowe, John E. Hough, Adam Geib, F. R. Bye, J. H. Liddell, Wm. Boyer, Samuel E. Young, George Rice, Wm. T. Elbin, Charles F. Leitz, George W. Warner, Frank E. Little, Thomas J. Shea, James McGuinness, Thomas Johnson, John J. Goodmanson, George W. Hammersley, Joseph E. Sweet, E. D. Holtz, William F. Roche, George Warner, John Bond, Joseph P. Ryan, J. T. Holmes, J. Newport Potts, John W. Steigerwald, William Upton, John F. Thomas, Samuel Wheeler, John J. McEvoy, Henry C. Mackie, R. S. Mooney, C. C. Speed, W. T. Keirle, John Wright, William H. Thompson.

Assistant Inspectors.—John A. Steiner, William H. Ebaugh, John H. Mitten, Jethro T. McCullough, H. P. Baldwin, Frank A. Lancaster.

SECOND DIVISION.

Charles T. Holloway, Marshal.

The second division of the parade was composed of volunteer firemen from out-of-town points, with our own veterans, with their ancient apparatus, heading the line.

Chief Holloway, with his silver speaking-trumpet and smiling face, at the head of his aids, led the division, with the Americus Band. Behind them came a barouche containing three of the vets knocked out by Father Time. They were Leml. S. Prince, aged 84, and William H. H. Turner, aged 78, who once ran with the old Independents in their palmy days, and Edward Horner, aged 85, one of the followers of the Columbia machine away back in the forties.

Marshal Holloway's aids were Gen. R. N. Bowerman, Henry Lutz, Capt. John H. Katzenberger, Augustus Albert, W. O. Beckenbaugh, W. J. Carroll, William P. Reilly, Robert St. J. Stewart, with a personal staff consisting of the visiting chief engineers and ex-chief engineers, assistant engineers and ex-assistant engineers, and officers and delegates representing fire associations from other cities.

The Baltimore veterans' float was in the front rank, and the old engines on it, odd-looking and strange as they were to those of this generation, were as familiar friends to their fathers and grandfathers. On the back part of the float was the "Grandfather," as the Vets affectionately call it—a little, old, battered hand engine, about six feet long and three feet high, built in 1764. It was discovered in a barnyard in Frederick about two years ago, and was afterwards brought to Baltimore with its companion, the Snake reel with its coil of copper-riveted leather hose, by the Frederick association and presented to the Baltimore veterans. The reel followed the float. Alongside the "Grandfather" on the float, and attended by four old firemen with their funny little oilcloth capes and hats that looked like tin buckets with brims to them, was the old Dolphin suction, painted like its ancient companion, in red and black, but it is a finer and more elaborate machine. Its upper works are supported at the corners by four bronze dolphins, and from these it took its name. It was the Mechanical Company's machine in the early days of that company, and years afterward it was found in Cambridge, where it had done efficient service. Above it floated the Columbia Company's banner of blue silk, with a painting on it representing a fireman rescuing a girl in her Sunday clothes from a burning building in the dead of the night. Below it was the motto, "To save from fire is our desire."

These were followed by the members of the association, walking six abreast, with their double-deck gallery engine "Fairy," drawn by four horses. This engine was originally owned by the Fairmount Company, of Philadelphia, and when built in 1845 was considered the finest engine in the country. The Fairmount veterans took part in the parade, and almost every one of them went up to take a look and affectionately stroke the machine that was once the pride of their city.

A little further on and hauled along by hand was the old engine of the Patapsco Company, "the Volunteer," which was rescued from a junk shop on Thames street some years ago by the venerable Peter Logue, who boasts of never having been in a theatre in his life.

The Veteran Volunteer Firemen's Association of Washington, with their hose carriage, the Hope Hose and Steam Fire Company, with their hose carriage, the Waterwitch Hook and Ladder Company, with handsome truck, and Friendship Company, No. 1, of Alexandria, Va., completed the first section.

The other companies of veterans in the division were the Veteran Volunteer Firemen's Association of Brooklyn, N. Y., who had a double-deck gallery engine, a sister to the Fairy of the Baltimore Vets.; the Active Association of Volunteer Firemen, of Philadelphia, and the Fairmount Company of Philadelphia, with their old red machine, built in 1791, decorated with steers' horns, and the motto, "Prompt to Action."

The Baltimore men had special pleasure in receiving their guests from a distance, two of whom were old "Baltimore boys." They were J. W. Kentzell and Henry A. Chase, of the Exempt Company, of San Francisco, and G. M. Ottinger, chief of the Salt Lake City fire department, who ran with the Deptford Company of Baltimore from 1854 to 1858. These, with Edward Koontz, President of the Juniors, of Frederick, Md., and W. T. Robinson, of Portsmouth, Va., were appointed special aids to Mashal Holloway.

A few of the companies had the ancient apparatus, now long out of use. The Winchester (Va.) boys, calling themselves the Sarah Zane Steam Fire Company, No. 1, had their original hand engine, a small double-decker, presented to them by their patron saint, Miss Sarah Zane, in 1840. The Hampton (Va.) boys, W. J. Weymouth in command, dragged the old Lafayette gallery suction along, and had a good time of it, too. This old engine was and still is a pretty good machine.

The Bay Ridge and Coney Island companies, of New York, hauled the old Deptford double-deck engine, which has, after a varied and useful career, returned to its home in Baltimore. When the company disbanded the engine was sold to a company in Frederick, who, after years of service, sold it to Winchester, Va., where it was discovered and bought by Mr. Holloway.

The Altoona boys, the Pennsylvania Railroad's firemen at Altoona, Pa., had the largest number of active men in line, and attracted a great deal of attention and no small amount of applause by their fancy marching.

The Catskill (N.Y.) boys were the dudes of the procession, and were remarkable for their uniformity of dress, their handsome appearance and their excellent marching. They were dressed in faultlessly fitting uniforms of fawn-colored cloth, and each man wore fawn-colored kid gloves and leather helmets of the same hue. They had with them their pretty hose carriage.

The Chambers Company, of Portsmouth, Va., with their fine band, received an ovation.

The other companies that took part in the parade were the Chemical Engine Company, No. 1, Manchester, Md.; Waterwitch Hose Company, No. 1, Port Deposit, Md.; Independent Fire Company, Annapolis, Md.; Reilly Hose Company, No. 1, Harrisburg, Pa.; Vigilant Fire Company, No. 1, York, Pa.; Phœnix Hose Company, Poughkeepsie, N. Y.; Active Association of Volunteer Firemen's Association, Philadelphia Pa.; Fame Hose Company, No. 1, Wilmington, Del.; Independent Fire Company, Portsmouth Va.; Bristol Fire Company, Bristol, Pa.; Frostburg Fire Company, Frostburg Md.; Fort Hamilton Fire Company, Fort Hamilton, N. Y.; Moyamensing Hook and Ladder Company, Chester, Pa.; Independent Fire Company, of Frederick, Md; American Hose and Hook and Ladder Company, Pennsylvania; Good Intent Fire Company, Pottsville, Pa.; The Good-Will Hook and Ladder Company, of Atlantic City, N. J. The majority of these brought their own bands with them, and the second division was probably the most musical in line.

THIRD DIVISION.

Samuel W. Regester, Marshal.

The third division was composed of officers of the modern city fire department, members of engine and truck companies, with apparatus and floats carrying chemical engine. The gallant firemen received their share of applause from the spectators, and deserved it all. The bearing of the men was free, steady, impressive. Wright's Band of 25 pieces preceded the division. The marshal of this division was one of Baltimore's Fire Commissioners.

FOURTH DIVISION.

Gen. Thomas J. Shryock, Marshal.

A gay tattoo was beaten upon the stones by the hoofs of the prancing horses as Gen. Thos. J. Shryock and his staff of seventy-six aids marched at the head of the fourth division. Gen.

Shryock has in several parades introduced novelties in the equipment of his aids, and he repeated his former efforts with splendid effect. The young men who composed his staff carried white riding crops, used a white bridle, and wore white kid gloves, white straw hats with white bands, dark cutaway coat, white vest, drab corduroy trowsers, and bronze medals struck at the Philadelphia mint. Thus attired upon their spirited horses they were received with applause. Henry R. Vonderhorst carried the white silken division colors, and John F. Schultz was bearer of the oriole colors.

The Uniformed Knights of the Golden Eagle were first in line, Lieut.-Gen. Louis E. Stilz, of Philadelphia, and his staff. Adjt.-Gen. J. Marple Hurtt, Inspector-Gen. Samuel M. Woods, Assistant Adjt.-Gen. Robert R. Hodge, Surgeon-Gen. Dr. J. E. Whiteford, with Col. James Billingsley, of Baltimore, and Col. Wilbur R. Rich, of Atlantic City, richly uniformed, marched in front of the Knights of the Golden Eagle drum corps, and Major B. M. Cross had immediate control of the Maryland Battalion, 150 men. The Supreme Chief of the order is Mr. R. Emory Enniss, of Baltimore, and with his staff, Grand Chief of the State N. S. M. Morton, Past Supreme Chief James Young and Past Chief Wm. Weaver, occupied carriages in the line. The Pennsylvania division was large. Brig.-Gen. M. C. Stafford and staff commanded it. Col. Steinbach had charge of the First Regiment, Col. Long of the Second and Col. Bigard of the Third. Unattached visiting Commanderies, among them Wilmington, (Del.) Washington and Philadelphia delegations, with bands, helped swell the ranks of the well-drilled and handsomely uniformed Knights.

The Knights of Pythias presented an imposing appearance, their broadcloth suits and elaborate gold and velvet regalia making them among the most conspicuous bodies in line. John A. Schwartz was in command of the Knights. Fraukenfield's West Philadelphia Band furnished marching music for them. Capt. Nicholas Tegges commanded the mounted Knights. Capt. Harry C. Cox had command of the Pythian Drill Association, No. 1; Capt. Harry Kemp, of Monumental, No. 2; Capt. John Block, of Baltimore, No. 3; P. H. Lenderking, of Maryland, No. 4; Capt. Edw. Appell, of Steuben, No. 5; Capt. Walter Hevern, of Ivanhoe, No. 6; Capt. Jesse G. Gosnell, of Druid, No. 7; Washington, No. 1, Nelson, No. 2, and Columbia, No. 3, of Washington; Wilmington, No. 1, of Wilmington, Rathbone, No. 8, of Alexandria, and Black Prince, No. 37, of New Freedom, Pa., were the visiting divisions.

The societies of St. George, St. Andrew and the Caledonian Society were represented in the division.

The Manual Training School placed eighty-five of its scholars in the procession, uniformed in white caps and yellow badges. A float carried specimens of the work of the scholars in wood, tin and metals.

Capt. Thos. P. Baldwin was in command of the Manual Training School and the public school pupils, the latter, 200 strong, in four divisions, being under the immediate command of James Young, Jr. Fifty colored Scholars marched proudly in rear of Capt Young's Division.

The Friendship Drum Corps headed the Order United American Mechanics, and Liberty Council, No. 24, turned out a goodly display.

Capt. A. G. Welsh, Jr., issued the orders to the Ellsworth Rifle Corps, which drilled with fine effect. The Cadets of Temperance followed, the Riverside Band of Port Deposit Md., preceding.

The Catholic Parochial schools contributed largely to the parade, and their neatly uniformed scholars were applauded all along the route. The Cadets of St. James School, little fellows all of them, wore a zouave uniform of blue and red, and with wooden guns presented the manual of arms drill with precision and promptness. Captain Harry Laritz was in command. St. Michael's Cadets, John Baier, captain, wore a uniform nearly similar and drilled in an admirable manner. St. John's Temperance Cadets, Captain Owen Kehler; Temperance Cadets of the Lady of Good Council, from Locust Point, Dominick Roche in command; the scholars of Calvert Hall, St. Joseph's Academy, marshaled by brothers of the institution; St. Peter's Temperance Cadets, St. Vincent's scholars, St. Alphonsus' school, the scholars from the Immaculate Conception, St. Patrick's, St. Joseph's, St. Mary's Star of the Sea, and St. Martin's scholars were all neatly uniformed in red caps, and some with sashes, and marched over the long route with unflagging steps. Brothers Quintian, Virgil and Julius rode in a carriage in rear of the school-boys.

For the Uniformed Catholic Knights Hoffman's Band was secured, and its martial airs marked the time for one of the largest and best drilled bodies in the parade. The Catholic Knights were out in force. Capt. Michael Lotz was in command, and back of him stretched a long line of societies, each fully uniformed. The societies were: Knights of St. Michael, Capt. John King; St. George, Capt. Antoine Schalitzky; St. Paul, Captain L. I. Ripple: St. Francis, Julius Hoffman; St. James, Capt. Andrew Shaffer; St. Wenceslaus, Capt. Joseph F. Shimanek; St. Vladislaus, Capt. Joseph Sibeski; St. Albert, Captain Schultz; St. Aloysius, Capt. John Flynn; St. Joseph, Capt. J. I. Gilchrist; St. Vincent, Captain J. A. Stewarts; St. Francis, (colored,) Capt. Smith; Latin Cross, Capt. Lawrence Mohr; St. Patrick, Capt Michael Keeney.

The display by St. Mary's Industrial School was one of the features. Two hundred boys, some small and some large, uniformed in gray suits trimmed with blue, and wearing blue caps, marched like veterans. The boys presented at the same time examples of their work. One float, 34 feet long, contained under arches of black and gold a printing press operated by a boy, and stocking knitting machines, at which three boys worked. Over the entire float were placed specimens of the labor of the scholars. The rear was filled with products of the garden and farm. A second float carried water and provisions for the boys, while a large vehicle contained all the trustees and the board of directors. Dr. R. H. Goldsmith commanded the division.

S. R. Jackson commanded the Patriotic Sons of America, who were accompanied by a float representing Washington at Valley Forge. The latter was unusually well executed. The Pennsylvania division of the Patriotic Sons of America participated with full ranks.

The order of the Shield of Honor was commanded by Wm. J. Cunningham. The Supreme Lodge, the Grand Lodge and various visiting lodges were in 33 open barouches, each member carrying an open Japanese parasol. The float of the Golden Eagles represented a widow seated beneath a canopy and two orphans, horns of plenty emptying their goods at their feet.

The floats of the benevolent organizations were features of a division so full of color and brilliancy as General Shryock's. That of the Golden Chain was one of the handsomest in the line. A number of tableaux showed the helping hand of the association keeping want from the widow and orphan. On a pedestal was a statue of a widow holding in her hand her husband's certificate of membership. On the rear of the float a large and exceedingly good representation of a cloud was constructed and from it an angel looked down upon another tableau of contented children.

The Catholic Benevolent Legion float helped to make the parade a success. It represented a room in which the amount of money for which a deceased husband was insured was being paid the widow.

The members of the Order of Iron Hall rode in carriages, and placed in line two elaborate floats.

The Royal Arcanum section was large, the members riding in carriages. A float of unique design, representative of the aims of the order, was entered in the line by it.

The front division was concluded with the W. H. Smith Drill Corps, colored, and the Veteran Corps, colored, the latter commanded by Capt. Jno. B. Briscoe.

The aids of Gen. Shryock were: A. E. Booth, F. C. Bolton, John Burns, Jr., Wm. W. Berry, Roger Barron, George W. Bartlett, R. H. Conway, Chas. Clark, A. J. Carr, Thomas A. Charsee, E. Pratt Callow, E. J. Dowell, Wm. Diffenderfer, J. J. Duffy, John R. Dorsey, T. A. B. Dukehart, Col. Patrick Duff, Wm. C. Ditman, Richard H. Diggs, Charles Dilworth, F. G. Evans, Robert Eccles, S. W. Frizzell, Achilles Ford, Edward Farland, J. Edward Duker, Arch. Anderson, A. Frank Gilbert, Wm. D. Gill, Jr., John Griffin, W. E. Guy, Dr. H. H. Goodman, G. F. M. Hauck, E. G. Hight, F. A. C. Hill, Dudley Helfrich, James Hutchinson, Wm. Howard, Chas. T. Harrison, Frank N. Hoen, W. W. Johnson, C. B. Kleibacker, John M. Keeler, James J. Kehoe, Henry Kroeger, Dr. A. B. Lyman, Charles A. Lucy, H. C. McAfee, J. H. Miller, Harvey McCoy,

Geo. R Medairy, S. R. Mason, Jas. C. Muller, Henry Mencken. R. Magruder, Charles M. Ness, William H. Ruby, Charles '. Ridgeley, Louis Reitz, Dr. Wm. Rickert, W. E. Sanders, Wm. S. Short, John F. Schultz, W. Warren Search, Leopold Schultz, James A. Smyser, George W. Starr, Carlos Sanchez, Charles Schmidt, S. A. Schwab, C. Shipley, Alonzo Thompson, George K. Thompson, Col. Richard B. Tippett, E. W. Taylor, James Thompson, Henry R. Vonderhorst, H. H. Vonderhorst, F. P. K. Walsh, Wm. M. Wilson, Wm. V. Wilson, and E. M. Wiley.

FIFTH DIVISION.

Col. Heinrich C. Tieck, Marshal.

Like a picture dropped from some Teutonic frame of medieval times was the grand display of the fifth or German division, marshaled by Col. Heinrich C. Tieck. His chief of staff was Parry Lee Downs, and his color-bearer Aug. F. Kaiser. Two lofty temples, 24 feet high, that gleamed with white and glinted from touches of gold, heralded from afar the Teutonic display, breathing in every touch the savor of fatherland, its song and art, its costume and its science, simplicity, sports and beverages.

After the marshal, his aids, four surgeons and the thirty special aids of the Germania Riding Club, clad in snowy breeches and helmets, black velvet jackets and leather leggins, came in advance of the ambulance, emblazoned with the red cross of Malta, without which no German procession is ever complete. It was in charge of Henry Bishop and was provided with stretcher, and plenty of ice, medicines, cordials and bandages. Then hove into full view the German-American float containing the temples, which represented "America and Germania United" with the advancement of their domains, as designed and constructed by Prof. Otto Fuchs.

Riding in advance came the mounted herald trumpeting aloud. Upon his head sat the puffed beretta and upon his form the gayly embroidered silk tunic of crimson and black and russet leggins Three noble women of the seventeenth century came next in the persons of Miss Mary Zaiser, Miss Nettie Zaiser, and Miss Lizzie Teipe, local horse women. They were dressed in satin trains and puffed sleeves, one wearing blue, one pink and the other purple richly embroidered. Upon their heads were Gretchen caps, studded with gems. Six gallant knights of brave Wallenstein's period rode after in velvet-slashed costumes, sleeves of blue satin, white felt hats, gilded sashes, broad silver buckles and swords. Six noble Huguenots in costume and six Land's knights, or knights guards were next and then the float of the United German Singers came.

It was ten feet broad and 36 feet long. On the front left corner was the American Indian in magnificent dress, and upon the other corner was the ancient Teuton in bear skins, with his horned fur cap. Next was a Gothic temple of white and gold, surrounded by four allegorical groups of art, poetry, music and science. A Raphael sitting at his easel with a bust beside him was the representative of art. A young lady dressed in classic Greek costume, reclining upon an antique seat, holding a tablet and pencil, and having a surrounding of books, the representation of poetry. Music was represented by a group of three ladies in Greek dress, one holding a lyre, the others playing upon double reed pipes. At the right was the savan of science, surounded by globe, telescopes and books. Within the temple, under an open canopy, sat Mother Ceres; before her were two wheat sheaves, and in her hands were sickel and flowers. Gay bannerettes ornamented the structure, together with shields and flags.

Then came the ocean waves, in which two globes floated. One showed America, the other Europe, and in each was a tall flagstaff, one having the American and the other the German flag. In the rear was a ledge of rocks upon which was an octagonal base, from which rose six marble columns supporting the dome of the United States Capitol. Within, in magnificent silk dresses, were Columbia with shield and Germania with the great sword, studded vest of armor and gold-jeweled crown. Upon the platform were shrubs, trees and flowers, while the graceful trimmings of the float were maroon and gold.

Attending this float were twelve medieval knights, guards of Lansquenets on foot, and behind came twelve more. Each of the six horses was draped in black, white and red—the German colors—and each was attended by a groom in broad white felt hat, brass collar and top boots.

Twenty carriages, the first of which contained President Louis Schneider, of the United Singers, with his condjutors. Louis Warkmeister, John Hoffmeister and Frederick Scheidt, followed, each bearing the pretty banner of one of the following societies: Baltimore Liederkranz, Harmonic, Germania Mænnerchor, Frohsin, East Baltimore Liederkranz, Arbeiter Mænnerchor, Baltimore Liedertafel, Arbeiter Liedertafel, Orpheus Mænnerchor, Thalia Mænnerchor, Canton Mænnerchor, Sængerrunde, Franz Abt Mænnerchor, Germania Mænnerchor Club, Baltimore Liederkranz Club, Concordia Club, German Orphan Asylum, General German Aged Men's Home.

The German shipping interest was displayed in great style. Officers under Captain Kuhlman, of the North German Lloyd steamship America, were followed by the Stevedores' Association, with a miniature of the America.

After carriages with officers of the organization came the big float of the *German Correspondent*. This was an Oriental temple of eight columns, trimmed with bannerettes, and having an arched top. Surrounding it were ten figurantes, representing every part of the globe from which the news comes At the rear were a half-dozen Africans in a grove of tropical plants. This concluded the first sub-division of the fifth division.

The second sub-division was composed of the fat, hearty-looking butchers in carriages or ahorse, with tall silk hats and white aprons. The horses drawing the butchers' floats had the significant motto, "Live and Let Live." It was evident that the butchers had carried out at least the first part of the motto. Their floats represented three stories. Upon the first were fat beeves, on the second calves good enough for a hundred prodigal sons. Above were sheep.

The third sub-division was mostly beer. There were plenty of floats and there was enough beer to float twice as many. The National Brewing Company and the Fort Marshal Brewery had warlike floats. The former was a monitor made of kegs, with a frowning turret from which protruded beer kegs for cannons, indicative, no doubt, of "shootin' 'em up." Each of its six horses was mounted by a colored man dressed in the spotless white United States navy uniform. Fort Marshal Brewery had a counterfeit of the old earthen fort that stood upon its site, and cannons were pointed toward the crowd. Nearly every float had a Gambrinus holding out the biggest five cent schooner in town.

The exhibit of the George Bauernschmidt Brewing Company was a practical idea of the way in which beer is manufactured. The float was a beer brewery in miniature, and contained an engine and boiler, steam kettle, mash tub, hop jack, hot and cold water tanks, surface cooler, Bartlett cooler, elevators and malt mill, the cellar where the beer casks are stowed, and the sample room, these latter being arranged in the rear of the float. The process of manufacturing beer was gone through in imitation of the real thing. The company had a tent at Pimlico, under which the float was on exhibition to the public. The float was 27 feet long, 10 feet wide and 22 feet high, and the lower part contained a fringe of canvas, on which was painted a scene of a cellar in a brewery, showing the manner in which the casks are stowed.

Vonderhorst & Son had a float giving typical scenes in beer brewing. It was an artistic exhibit. The centre of the float contained a thirty-five-barrel beer cask. Roosting upon this was an immense carved eagle, six feet six inches from tip of tail to point of beak, holding a large gilded V in the mouth. This is the trade-mark of the firm. On each side and in rear of the float were the heads of beer barrels. On each side of the forward part were heads of Gambrinus, done in plaster of Paris and cement and painted. Each of these was mounted on shields of the United States and held a white streamer floating from the eagle's beak. Each beer barrel was decorated with a wreath of cedar, and surrounding the Gambrinus heads were sheaves of barley. Over the large cask were entwined malt vines to represent how the plant grows.

The brewery of J. F. Wiesner turned out a float with a crimson plush throne, canopied by the Maryland colors and a background of red, white and blue. A Gambrinus sat there. At his feet, under a golden eagle, sat two ladies in decollete style, personating the Goddess of Liberty and Germania. Before these were beer barrels, around which were green hop vines. Gambrinus held an immense silver cup.

George Brehm's float was a rock grotto, with brick arches, from which rose a tall castellated watch-tower. Polished kegs —beer kegs, of course—and a big barrel filled it up, the driver was on the barrel.

While others had a practical illustration of brewing beer, John Bauernschmidt, Jr., had a still more practical one, of drawing beer. Three barrels with operative spigots were moistening the crowd and keeping the parade from becoming a dry show.

Darley Park had an Eiffel tower with barreled dampness at every landing.

The Globe brewery had a float as tasteful as its Munich beer. A tremendous cask handsomely painted rested upon an immense rock, and a golden globe surmounted the whole.

The Baltimore Brewing Company had a series of steps filled with little girls in white dresses, who whiled away the tedium of the procession by drinking pop. At the top was Gambrinus with a page in handsome costume.

George Guenther had a chariot drawn by bock goats, which Gambrinus was driving, with a fresh keg from a cool grotto.

Bayview had four big schooners full of mock beer with cotton foam.

Engel, Kirchheimer & Regnier, coppersmiths, had a big steam jack gayly painted with emblems of the brewing business.

Following the floats were brewmasters driving in barouches.

The Onkel Braesig Verein was redolent of the North German's beloved Low Germany. Onkel Braesig himself, the patron of the nation, sat before just such a straw thatched structure with concrete walls as many adopted Americans were born under. Dressed in the long brown Hanoverian coat capped with fur, knee breeches and leggins, he was accompanied by his favorite nieces, Minnekin and Linnekin, as so beautifully related by the revered poet Fritz Reuter, the bard of the Low Germans.

The other float was the one showing the village lads and lassies going to the Kirmess dressed in their native costumes. The lads wore broad white collars, red suspenders, knee breeches, straw broadbrims and gay ties. The floats were decorated exactly as in village Deutschland, with gilt and colored paper.

The societies of the Black Knights, Order of Harugari, and Dr. Martin Luther Sick Benefit Association concluded this sub-division.

In the fourth and last sub-division were the Sons of Bohemia, with Louis Benick, marshal, and aids, F. J. Ruzicka, John Proley, M. Benech, Joseph Lebeda, F. Shimek, Thomas Kudril, K. Feter, Jos. Jerabeck, D. Zelenka, John Payril, A. Sesula, Jos. Feilman, Jacob Weis, K. Hurt.

The Bohemia Gymnastic Association, in neat blue blouses,

black trowsers and black Alpine hats, were followed by the Bohemian "Casino" Pleasure Assembly and lodges of the C. B. P. S. and C. S. P. O. The Bohemian Young Men's Association Hoczde concluded the fifth division.

The following were the aids to Marshal Heinrich C. Tieck: Col. Parry Lee Downs, chief of staff; August F. Kaiser, division color-bearer.

Aids.—John W. H. Fry, Col. John C. Horstmeier, Henry Brehm, A. C. Schmidt, Herman Kluth, J. T. Graceu, B. B. Ottenheimer, Geo. C. Jeiser.

Surgeons.—Dr. Amos L. Gage, Dr. John C. Hemmeter, Dr. Jos. C. Ohlendorf, Dr. P. G. Dill.

Special Aids—Germania Riding Club, Maj. Frederick Bauernschmidt, commanding; August J. Heise, adjutant; George Bauernschmidt, Jr., guidon-bearer.

Andrew Mueller, Rudolph Vollmer, John E. Harting, Otto Ahrens, Henry Merz, Jacob Klein, John C. Becken, August Hengemihle, Charles H. Mueller, George Leimbach, August Danzeglock, Henry Eppler, Henry Bishop, Chas. Quast, Chas. Beck, J. F. Barclay, Wm Balke, John Marsch, Morris Brooks, Wm. T. Auer, Achelis Ford, John H. Horst, Albert L. Herford, Edw. Umbach, Otto Hellwig, Oscar Goeger, Charles A. Lerian, Charles Werner.

SIXTH DIVISION.

Major J. G. Pangborn, Marshal.

An almost interminable line of floats and business wagons that were a mass of brilliant colors, an exhibition of nearly every conceivable manufactured product, with numerous illustrations of the process of manufacture, together with beautiful, artistic and allegorical representations, the whole interspersed with bands of music and attended with the greatest enthusiasm—such was the trades display. The various firms entered into the affair with such enthusiasm and were so lib eral in expending money to decorate their floats that the result could not have been otherwise than creditable.

The floats were built in the workshops or yards of the firms, and when constructed were usually too large and unwieldy to be removed bodily to the street. On this account they were built in sections, and when completed were dismantled, to be reconstructed just prior to starting for the parade. This work was begun at midnight Sunday, and in a number of cases was barely completed in time to join the procession.

The display occupied the sixth division and was the longest in the whole parade. It was under the direction of Major J. G. Pangborn, chief marshal, who rode on horseback in front, with Col. Wm. A. Boykin, chief of staff. Among the bands in this section were the United States Marine Band, the Naval Academy Band, Fourth Pennsylvania Regiment Band and Philadelphia City Drum Corps, Maryland Cornet Band, Chesapeake City Band, Burgoyne's Band, Americus Piccolo Band, United

States Artillery Band, Annapolis Cornet Band, Emmerton Band and Baltimore Drum Corps. Each section was preceded by its color-bearer and had its chief, with his aids. The order of the display was as follows:

RAILROAD, EXPRESS, STEAMSHIPS.

Twenty file front of B. and O. conductors, uniformed employes B and O. R. R. Co., J. Van Smith, commander; floats of the B. and O. R. R., U. S. Express Co., uniformed employes P. R. R., J. A. Wilson, commander; floats of the P. R. R., Adams Express Co., Baltimore City Passenger Railway, People's Passenger Railway, Furness Steamship Line, Edward Mitchell; Combined Sailmakers.

PRINTING, NEWSPAPERS, LITHOGRAPHY.

Floats of Baltimore Typographical Union, No. 12, six in number, illustrative of the progress of the "art preservative."

Float of "THE BALTIMORE TELEGRAM," representing a family scene—the interior of a library—with family engaged in reading Baltimore's great weekly and working out the puzzles. The horses were blanketed with unique advertisements of James Young, the Printer.

DRY GOODS, NOTIONS, HAT INDUSTRY.

Combined Wholesale Dry Goods, Straw Hat Manufacturers, Armstrong, Cator & Co., Hurst, Purnell & Co., Hodges Bros., Daniel Miller & Co., Witz, Biedler & Co., Johnson, Sutton & Co., Pearre Bros. & Co , Rouse, Hempstone & Co., Chesapeake Shirt Company, Wise Bros., S. Blum & Son; John A. Griffiths & Co., E. Pohl & Co., W. J. O'Neal.

DRESS GOODS, FANCY GOODS, MILLINERY.

Joel Gutman & Co , C. Simon & Son, Posner Bros., S. Kann & Sons, E. Rosenthal, L. Krauss.

NURSERIES, AGRICULTURAL IMPLEMENTS.

Combined Florists, William Corse & Sons, Robert Cremens, Baltimore Farm Implement Company.

PIANOS, PICTURES, GOLD LEAF.

William Knabe & Co., Charles M. Stieff, Schneider & Fuchs, McCaddin & McElwee, Adam Deupert.

CLOTHING, FURNISHING GOODS, MERCHANT TAILORING.

Oehm's Acme Hall, New York Clothing House, Strasburger & Son, Likes, Berwanger & Co., H. Wurtzburger & Son, Isaac Benesch.

HOUSEHOLD GOODS, PAPER HANGING.

Hecht & Sons, Joseph Scherer,, American Sewing Machine Company, Louis Kaufman, Mrs V. Schlenth, Aug Hengemihle.

TEAS, COFFEE, SALT.

Martin Gillet & Co., C. D. Kenny, Alex. Kerr, Bro. & Co., H. A. Hosmer & Bro.

LITHOGRAPHY, PRINTING, PAPER.

Isaac Friedenwald, Ronemous & Co., Goldsmith & Runkle.

LEATHER, HARNESS, SADDLERY.

Shoe and Leather Board of Trade, Lerch Bros., O. F. Day & Co., H. O. Naerger.

FURNITURE, UPHOLSTERY, MANTELS.

Atlantic Furniture Co., M. L. Straus & Co., Uriah A. Pollock, Broadway Furniture Co., Baltimore Furniture Co., Isaac Benesch, The Reliable Furniture Co., Jno. C. Weems & Bro., Riddle & Williams, John C. Scherer, Jr., F. X. Ganter, Geo. D. Magruder, M. Tregor & Co., The Sauer Mfg. Co.

TIN-WARE, STOVES, PLUMBING.

Matthai, Ingram & Co., Keen & Hagerty, S. B. Sexton & Son, The Keely Stove Co., Master Plumbers' Association.

GROCERIES, BAKING POWDER, SOAP.

Chris. Lipps, Union Soap Co., H. Cone & Sons, P. New & Sons, Patapsco Baking Powder Co., Fruit Puddine Co., Reid & Co., Empire Steam Laundry, Brexton Laundry, F. Sauerwein.

ICE, CANNED GOODS, PRODUCE.

The Ice Exchange, Cochran-Oler Co., Jacob Frederick & Son, John Biemiller, Terry, Lara & Co., Consumers' Ice Co., Sumwalt Ice Co., Wm. Numsen & Sons, J. Wm. Ports, Fairbanks Canning Co., T. C. Pugh & Co., S. L. McCully, G. Cassard & Son, Wm. S. Duffy, John Dumbler, B. O. Frizzle.

TOBACCO, WINES, LIQUORS.

L. H. Neudecker, The Gottschalk Co., Samuel Hois, Netter Bros., Jacob Schild, S. Kann, Adam J. Gossman.

BREAD, CRACKERS, CONFECTIONERY.

Jas. D. Mason & Co., Geo. Blome & Son, Geo. R. Skillman, Rice Bros., J. W. Cruett, Baltimore Pie Co.

DRUGS, MEDICINES, CHEMICALS.

Lilly, Rogers & Co., Muth Bros., The Chas. A. Vogeler Co., Kohler Medicine Co., A. S. Shaffer, G. S. McGreevy.

FLOUR, FEED, FERTILIZERS.

The C. A. Gambrill Co., Tate, Hinrichs & Co., E. N. Gardner & Co., Rinehart, Childs & Co., Chemical Co. of Canton, M. Murray Brooks & Co., M. J. & W. A. Brown, Jas. R. Clark & Company.

POTTERY, CEMENT, MARBLE.

Employes of The Maryland Pottery Co., floats of The Maryland Pottery Co., C. C. McColgan & Co., Charles E. Ehman, J. M. Witzgall, White Bronze Co.

TOYS, BABY CARRIAGES, FIREWORKS.

Edw. S. Prior & Co., Carriage and Toy Co., William Bond, Wm. T. Sagle.

GLASS, PAINTS, BRUSHES.

Combined Glass Manufacturers, Baker Bros. & Co., Swindell Bros, Henry Seim & Co, L. Bokemeyer, G. & N. Popplein, Hirshberg, Hollander & Co., Crown Brush Works, Maryland White Lead Works.

MACHINERY, SAFES, BUILDERS' SUPPLIES.

E. J. Codd Co., Reuter & Mallory, Clarence M. Kemp, L. H. Miller, John Scherer & Son, Coil Steam Cleaning Co.

CARRIAGES, WAGONS, LUMBER.

Hartman & Moore, Moses McCormick & Bro, J. Richey Wilson, J. L. Gilbert & Bro., W. S. Taylor & Co., H. E. Cook & Bro., J. R. Sagle.

ELECTRICITY, TELEGRAPH, CABLE.

Postal Telegraph and Cable Company, horseback riders and floats of Postal Telegraph Co., Viaduct Mfg. Co., Electric Illuminating Co.

SECTION CHIEFS AND AIDS.

The chiefs of sections were B. F. Bond, E. V. Hermange, Samuel Tregallis, Louis K. Gutman, James Pentland, George N. Appold, Fred. Henneman, Thomas G. Speights. James E. Byrd, William Deutsch, H. A. Lerch, Col. Louis Strasburger, W. H. Matthai, Jacob Murbach, Wesley Oler, L. H. Neudecker. H. L. Washburn, Harry A. Devries, E. T. Rinehart, Chas. L. Baker, Charles K. Ober, N. Popplein, Clarence M. Kemp, J. Richey Wilson and T. M. Dunn.

The aids to Chief Marshal Pangborn were Col. R. Stockett Mathews, F. R. Biedler, A. Bechoffer, John T. Gray, William Hunt, R. W. Eddins, W. D. Platt, Edward Futvoye, Isaac Guggenheimer, J. L. Gilbert, P. N. Green, David Herring, J. M. Ingram, Joseph F. Matthai, Thomas C. Pugh, Dr. B. Holly Smith, Samuel A. Pitt, L. C. Rice, S. B Sexton, Jr., Ed. P. Suter, Thomas N. Terry. Jerome Vogeler, George R. Webb, H. P. C. Wilson, Louis Warrington, William Wiedley, A. L. Straus, John W. Linton, A. L. Frederick, George A. Albaugh, L. C. Byrd, J. F. H. Wyse, J. R. Wilson, L. Tallerman, E. Clay Timanus, J. A. Wilson, J. D. Wade, J. W. Schaur, A. D. Seeman, G. D. Sewell, Henry Schafer, Walter R. Sweeney, W. L. Stansberry, Oscar E. Rice, E. Rosenfeld, J. B. Richardson, Edward Rosenthal, W. D. Randall, E. L. Raborg, G. T. Rappainer, C. W. A. New, Harry Nicodemus, Edward Noel; Samuel Nixdorff, J. T. Plummer, E. J. Parsons, Jr., H. S. Dulaney, Gabriel Duval, Walter Dawson, J. M. Davis. M. J. Tyson, Frank Dorn, Frank N. Dawes, W. G. O'Brien, Theo. Beimiller, Grason Bramble, A. Benesch, J. M. Boone, J. L. Boone, Samuel Bass, Frederick Burger, W. R. Birch, H. A. Malthan, Harry Muller, E. S. Merriam, E. J. McCleary, Charles G. Campbell, W. H. Cockey, George H. Clogg, G. A. Cook, H. E. Cook, E. Coulson, C. C. Collmus, Edward Lipps, F. W. Lipps, C. W. Lewis, S. T. Earle, N. Everhart, C. R. Kendig, J. C. Krautz, A.

A. Kayser, George Keeler, Wm. Kress, J. A. Fritter, William Fraser, J. W. Geiger, F. C. Gardner, W. H. Gibbons, James Bonn, Louis Houghton, Wm. P. Hall, John Hood, W. J. Herring, William P. Hall, S. O. Heiskell, C. G. Hill, J. Parker Hynds, C. A. Heman, Irving Hellen, Ed. Hecht, W. H. Hess, John Harris, C. C. Jones, H. E. Jackins, Fred. Dreschler, William Thom.

SECOND DAY—TUESDAY.

Horse and cattle sales at Pimlico, 10 to 12 A. M.
Awarding of premiums for horses and cattle at Pimlico.
Hand fire engine test, 10 A. M, on Mt. Vernon Place.
Races at Pimlico, 1 P. M.
Parade of Knights, 2 P. M.
Tournament at Pimlico, 5 P. M.
Ball in open pavilion at Pimlico after tournament.

THIRD DAY—WEDNESDAY.

Horse and cattle sales at Pimlico, 10 to 12 A. M.
Awarding of premiums in household, agricultural implement and other departments at Pimlico.
Races at Pimlico, 3 P. M.

FOURTH DAY—THURSDAY.

Parade of labor organizations, 9.30 A. M.
Horse and cattle sales at Pimlico, 10 to 12 A. M.
Labor meeting and addresses at Pimlico.
Representation of battle of North Point at Pimlico, 2 P. M.
Vocal concert preceding battle.
Dedication of new postoffice, 8 P. M.
Maryland ball, Concordia Opera House, 9.30 P. M.

FIFTH DAY—FRIDAY.

Parade of soldiers, 9 A. M. Reviewed by Governor Jackson and Governors of other States.
Horse and cattle sales at Pimlico, 10 to 12 A. M.
Races at Pimlico, 3 P. M.
Bombardment of Fort McHenry, 8 P. M.

SIXTH DAY—SATURDAY.

Horse and cattle sales at Pimlico, 10 to 12 A. M.
Races at Pimlico, 3 P. M.

www.ingramcontent.com/pod-product-compliance
Lightning Source LLC
Chambersburg PA
CBHW020059170426
43199CB00009B/338